Milk Jar Cookies

BAKEBOOK

Milk Jar Cookies

BAKEBOOK

Cookies, Cakes, Pies, and More for Celebrations and Every Day

COURTNEY COWAN

Photography by
ASHLEY MAXWELL

RIZZOLI
NEW YORK

Contents

INTRODUCTION *7*

HELPFUL HINTS
AND PREFERRED PRODUCTS *11*

Cookies

Chocolate Chip Cookies *15*

White Chocolate Raspberry Cookies *17*

Chocolate Chip Walnut Cookies *21*

Chocolate Chocolate Chip Cookies *23*

White Chocolate Macadamia Cookies *27*

Banana Split Cookies *29*

Cinnamon Sugar Cookies *33*

Rocky Road Cookies *35*

Oatmeal Raisin Cookies *39*

Chocolate Pecan Caramel Cookies *43*

Salted Butterscotch Cookies *45*

Mint Chocolate Cookies *49*

Key Lime Pie Cookies *51*

Waffle Cookies *55*

Pumpkin Pie Cookies *57*

Chocolate-Covered Banana Cookies *61*

Peanut Butter Cookies *63*

Picnic Cookies *67*

Apple Oatmeal Cookies *69*

English Toffee Cookies *73*

Milk and Cereal Cookies *75*

Lemon Blueberry Cookies *79*

Peach Cobbler Cookies
with Streusel Topping *81*

Chocolate-Covered Strawberry Cookies *85*

Peppermint Bark Cookies *87*

Cakes and Bakes

Your New Favorite Chocolate Cake
with Chocolate Fudge Frosting *91*

Chocolate Chip Cookie Cake *94*

Better Than Almost Anything Cake *97*

Confetti Cake
with White Frosting *101*

Carrot Cake
with Cream Cheese Frosting *103*

Perfectly Fudgy Brownies *107*

Cheesecake
with Cherry Compote Topping *109*

Strawberry Shortcake *111*

Hazel's German Chocolate Cake
with Coconut Pecan Frosting *115*

Pies

The Perfect Piecrust	*119*
Mixed Berry Pie	*121*
Apple Pie	*125*
Pumpkin Pie	*126*
Pecan Pie	*129*

No Bake Treats

Butterscotch Pudding *with* Homemade Whipped Cream	*130*
Chocolate Pudding *with* Crème de la Cloud	*133*
Banana Split Puppy Chow	*136*
Hoosier Haystacks	*139*
PB&J Krispy Treats	*140*
Chocolate-Covered Pretzels	*143*
Banana Pudding *with* Vanilla Wafer Cookies	*144*
Marshmallows	*147*
Chocolate Fudge	*150*
Tapioca Pudding	*153*

Breakfast Bakes

Sour Cream Coffee Cake	*154*
Pumpkin Bread	*157*
Mama's Cinnamon Rolls	*161*
Aunt Suz's Banana Nut Bread	*163*
Blueberry Streusel Muffins	*167*
Bacon Cheddar Scones	*169*
Mrs. Z's Chocolate Chocolate Chip Zucchini Bread	*173*
Lemon Ricotta Pancakes *with* Blueberry Compote	*175*
Banana Split Waffles	*179*
Amanda's Grief Biscuits	*180*
Sweet and Spicy Corn Muffins	*183*
Lemon Poppy Seed Muffins	*184*

ACKNOWLEDGMENTS *187*

INDEX *188*

Introduction

Dear baker,

In the summer of 2012, I was not outside cartwheeling in the perennial Los Angeles sunshine. Instead, I was bed-ridden. Or I suppose "couch-ridden" is a better term, since the TV was in the living room and the Olympics were a twenty-four-hour-a-day-distraction. I was recovering from back surgery—a last-ditch effort in a long line of attempted fixes for my spine. I had been a gymnast throughout my early life, and at one point I was even good enough to have a shot at training for the national team, but the sport was too hard on my body. So there I was, thirty-four years old, recovering but mostly dreaming of what could have been while watching the USA gymnastics team win gold in London. Sometimes life can have a funny sense of humor.

I'm telling you this story because, as odd as the time and place may seem, that was where Milk Jar Cookies began. Hanging over the mantle near the TV was a banner I had made for my wedding a few years earlier. In paisley fabric letters, it read, **"Life's Short, Eat Cookies."** I don't know if it was the inspiration I felt watching the Fierce Five win medal after medal, or the serious medication I was on, but I realized I was ready to go for it. You see, I had spent the previous seven years pursuing my dream of owning a cookie company, but only as a side hustle while I worked full-time as a television producer. But there, laid up on that couch, I realized what I wanted to do with my life, and I started writing a business plan for what would become Milk Jar Cookies.

The thing I love about baking is that it has the ability to spread joy in three distinct ways: one, to the baker while doing the delicious work; two, seeing, smelling, and tasting the fruits of your labor; and three, sharing your baked goods with others. It's like a three-pronged happiness fork! The physical act of baking has an intense power to change a mood, relieve stress, heal a broken heart. Measuring ingredients, mixing, getting your hands sticky with dough is a joyful, therapeutic experience. If you don't believe me, try it (that's why you're here, right?). And, the sugary, joyous dopamine hit of eating a treat has a way of briefly hitting the pause button on the day's worries. Then, to be on the receiving end of a delightful treat? Well, that's just magic for everyone. Baking for others is one of the purest expressions of love. It's the first thing we think to do when someone is sad or happy; whether commiserating or celebrating, adding cookies, cake, or a pie to the mix is the thing we do.

People often ask me, "Why cookies?" and my immediate thought is, "Why not?"

However, over the years I've discovered a more meaningful answer to that question. For me, cookies have always been *it*. Like many of us, the first thing I learned to bake was cookies, and I have fond kitchen memories of sneaking raw cookie dough with my sister behind my mom's back. When I wasn't doing gymnastics, you could find me making cookies. As I grew up and developed my own cookie recipes, I realized these chunks of doughy goodness were not held to the same standard as other desserts. They were not seen as "gourmet," or a special treat to bring to a dinner party, and certainly not works of art. And I knew that was a missed opportunity, because my cookie recipes were well-thought-out chemistry experiments, each ball of dough hand-crafted and appointed like any confection you would find in the pages of *Bon Appétit* magazine. I wanted to elevate the classics, in particular the chocolate chip cookie, and create a version worthy of both the adults who crave something truly special and the kids who just want their sugar quota—a cookie work of art.

After years of tinkering, I finally landed on the recipe that would eventually become Milk Jar Cookies's famous Chocolate Chip Cookie. With a balanced sweetness, a delightfully crisp outer edge, and doughy center, my cookies became popular with friends, family, and coworkers; people often mistook them for store-bought. I started thinking I might be onto something! So began months of experimenting with different cookie flavors in the kitchen of my one-bedroom apartment. As a single girl in my twenties, I had lots of time to dedicate to this delicious hobby of mine and I let my imagination run wild. I developed a full menu of cookie flavors, inventing future classics like

Banana Split and Rocky Road Cookies; and in 2005, I started a cookie company that I affectionately named Sweet Cheeks Cookies after the pet name I had for my sister, Holly. While I continued to work full-time in television, I grew my online business out of my coat closet.

What began as a creative outlet quickly grew into my full-fledged passion. My new dream became to open a brick-and-mortar cookie shop and reinvent the experience of eating a cookie: a quality product presented beautifully on vintage china, served in an inviting storefront, elevating a simple moment into a celebration. Finally, in the spring of 2013, I opened Milk Jar Cookies with that mission in mind. I knew I had something special when we sold out by 2:00 p.m. on the day of our soft opening. We then tried to over-prepare for our grand opening, only to sell out even earlier in the day. The rest of that afternoon, people were clamoring at the door like zombies. And the company has been growing ever since. I have always been grateful that our single biggest challenge is meeting the demand.

Seven years later and after millions of cookies served, Milk Jar Cookies is now a brand synonymous with delectability, friendliness, and excellence, and a destination for those seeking a little pop of joy. Even though we're situated in L.A., a city known for its healthy culture, our customers have come to fully embrace our motto: ***Life's Short, Eat Cookies***.

After seeing the response to my cookies, I knew I wanted to bring the Milk Jar experience into home kitchens, allowing people to experience all three prongs of joy that baking elicits. Now, here you are, holding this book in your soon-to-be-flour-covered hands. In the pages that follow, I will weave personal stories of the people, places, and inspiration behind my favorite recipes, together with a host of baking tips and a visual feast of the accessible process and the delightful, doughy rewards. While cookies are the singular focus of my business, I love to bake everything, and I've included lots of other recipes that warm the soul just as much. From cakes to pies to quick no-bake treats, there is a recipe in here fit for any occasion or just a Tuesday. With an approachability that leaves double boilers and hard-to-find tools behind, I hope this book serves as a guidepost for even the most novice bakers and a catalyst for happy times in the kitchen.

To be honest, since opening Milk Jar Cookies, I've suffered from that eternal entrepreneurial struggle of finding a balance between life and work. One aspect of my pre–Milk Jar life that had gone by the wayside was "baking for fun." Writing this cookbook allowed me to rediscover the joy of baking for myself (and not only because there are orders to fill), revisiting my old favorites and developing a few new ones. The process of researching, experimenting, getting it wrong, and trying again until the recipe was my version of "perfect" reaffirmed what I've known along—baking is magic. So thank you, dear reader, for making it all possible.

I can't wait for you to get started and bake up some happy in your very own kitchen. The final thing to know before you turn the page is that no baking session is complete without some rockin' tunes. My mother instilled in me the love of music, and I'm quite certain that

dancing around the kitchen, singing loudly into your spatula, improves the final product. I'm known at the shop for curating my own playlists, and throughout this book, you'll find QR codes that will lead you to special playlists I've created for you to help you make the most of your baking experience. We're in this together, and I'd love to follow your baking journey. Upload your pictures and videos and tag them with @courtneykcowan and #milkjarbakebook so I can see your creations and the smiles that follow. Now, crank the tunes, dive in, and have FUN!

Love,
Courtney

Helpful Hints and Preferred Products

GENERAL NOTES

While many of my cookie recipes have the same base dough, I have chosen to go through the step-by-step process for each and every flavor to simplify your experience. This way, you can decide what flavor you want to make, turn to that page, and hit the ground running. Who has time to flip back and forth when there's sweets to bake?

Always read the recipe from start to finish before you begin. This will allow you to be completely prepared and have a smoother baking experience. Oftentimes, ingredients need to be a certain temperature or the timing is otherwise sensitive, so knowing what's coming is always helpful. If you can go a step further and pre-measure your ingredients, smooth sailing ahead!

Measure precisely. Baking is all about chemistry, and every morsel of every ingredient contributes to the final product, so take your time and measure exactly.

Presentation matters. I believe that beautiful things taste better, so taking a few extra minutes to sculpt each cookie by hand or get creative with a piecrust is one of the highlights of baking for me. And don't let the beauty stop there. Serving your treats on pretty dishes instead of paper plates or napkins adds another level of enjoyment. If you don't already own a couple of vintage saucers, platters, and cake stands, I recommend checking out your local thrift stores and flea markets. They can be amazing and affordable places to bring a little fancy home on a budget.

INGREDIENTS

BUTTER: I have always preferred to use unsalted butter and then add salt when needed, so all of the recipes in this book call for unsalted butter.

BUTTERMILK: This is super easy to make on the fly. Just add 1 tablespoon of fresh lemon juice or vinegar to 1 cup of whole milk, stir, and wait 15 minutes. Voilà! Buttermilk.

CHOCOLATE CHIPS: I use semisweet chocolate chips exclusively in my baking, as I prefer the taste. Feel free to use whatever variety you like best. And, after all these years, I am still a Toll House girl. Dance with the one that brung ya, right?

COCOA POWDER: When choosing a cocoa powder, make sure that you are using unsweetened 100-percent natural cocoa powder. Several recipes in this book call for a combination of regular and dark cocoa powders

to get a rich chocolate flavor and that dramatic dark color. If you don't have both on hand, just add the amounts together and use the one you have for the total.

EGGS: A couple of notes about eggs: 1) all of the cookie recipes call for extra-large eggs, as they contain a bit more egg white. If you only have large eggs, use two eggs plus one egg white, and 2) when a recipe requires room temperature eggs, you can leave them on the counter for 30 minutes or run them under warm water for 3 minutes if you're short on time. Eggcellent!

FLAVORED EXTRACTS: I am a big fan of baking with pure flavored extracts, and I buy them all online from a company named OliveNation. Their products are high quality and the selection sends my imagination into overdrive, often inspiring new creations.

FLOUR: Unless otherwise stated, all of the flour called for in the recipes is all-purpose. I prefer to use unbleached, but as long as you're using all-purpose, you're good to go.

GLUTEN-FREE FLOUR: I have experimented with a bunch of gluten-free flours over the years and even tried mixing my own at one point (a rather expensive undertaking), but when Cup4Cup finally hit the market, all of my gluten-free baking struggles disappeared. It is such a wonderful product that doesn't change the taste of your treat and bakes up beautifully. I find that adding an additional 1½ teaspoons per cup of flour called for in a recipe allows the gluten-free version to bake in a way that's consistent with the gluten-full one.

PEANUT BUTTER: I'm choosy, so I choose Jif. While I believe there is a place in this world for unsweetened peanut butters, baking is not it. Let's live on the edge and use the sugary ones we were raised on. That being said, I will take a slightly grown-up stance and say that Jif Natural is top-notch, and I approve of your use of it in my recipes.

SHORTENING: I like to use a combination of fats in a lot of my baked goods, so you'll need shortening on hand. I prefer to use Spectrum Organics All Vegetable Shortening, which you can find at many grocers and online.

TAPIOCA PEARLS: To make the Tapioca Pudding recipe, you'll need large #40 tapioca pearls, which I like to order online from Hoosier Hill Farm. Maybe it's because they come from my home state of Indiana, but I think they're the best.

VANILLA EXTRACT: While I prefer the rich, creamy flavor of Madagascar vanilla over other varieties, the one thing I will never compromise on is that it must be pure extract, not imitation. These days, the price of vanilla has gotten pretty steep, but it is worth every penny when crafting your goodies.

YOGURT CHIPS: The sweet, creamy tang of yogurt chips is the key to a few of the recipes in the pages that follow. Sometimes, you can find these at the grocery store, but if you can't, I recommend ordering them from OliveNation.

EQUIPMENT

BAKING SHEETS AND PANS: I'm surprisingly not incredibly picky when it comes to my baking sheets and pans, and you can get really good ones inexpensively. The recipes in the following pages call for regular baking sheets, bread loaf pans, a 9-inch springform pan, 8 by 8-inch brownie pan, 9-inch cake pans, and a muffin tin. All of these can be found at any department or home goods store.

MIXING BOWLS: I highly recommend having two different kinds of mixing bowls on hand. First, I love my set of plastic KitchenAid nesting bowls that have nonslip bottoms and pour spouts, both of which help keep the messes to a minimum. Second, a set of heat-resistant glass bowls will come in handy when melting chocolate and making some of the recipes that require hot ingredients.

PARCHMENT PAPER: When it comes to keeping treats from sticking, I always line my baking sheets and pans with parchment paper. While you can buy a roll of it and cut it as needed, I find it much easier to purchase a box of pre-cut sheets to fit baking sheets and cake pans. My go-to site for purchasing is The Smart Baker. In addition to lining the bottom with parchment paper, make sure you still grease the sides of your cake and bread pans.

PIE PANS: I bake exclusively with ceramic pie pans, as they conduct heat evenly for that perfectly baked crust. There are also so many beautiful pie pan options that will dress up your pies! All of the recipes in this book make 10-inch pies, so if you are using a 9-inch pan, you might have a little extra filling.

STAND MIXER: While most of the recipes in this book can be made with a hand mixer, there are a few that are very difficult without a stand mixer (I'm looking at you, Marshmallows). If you don't have a stand mixer and march forward with a hand mixer, note that it might take a little longer than is noted in the recipe.

CHOCOLATE CHIP COOKIES

When I was a kid, I made chocolate chip cookies at least once a week. My mom taught me the basics of baking, and this was my go-to activity with my sister and friends who would sleep over. Some might say I was obsessed. One fateful night in my eleventh year, we were out of baking soda, and I thought, "Eh, it's only a teaspoon, it can't make that big a difference," and I carried on with my cookie mission. How wrong I was. That was the night I learned that baking is a science and each ingredient has its role to play. I was fascinated! So began years of experimenting with different ingredients until I landed upon the recipe that became the cornerstone for Milk Jar Cookies. My desire was a well-balanced flavor that was wasn't overly sweet and was baked with that perfectly crisp outer layer and doughy center. All these years later, there is still nothing like the delicious satisfaction of sitting down with one of my warm chocolate chip cookies and a tall glass of ice-cold milk.

Makes 15 to 18 three-inch cookies

4 cups all-purpose flour	1 cup sugar
1 teaspoon baking soda	1 cup packed light brown sugar
1 teaspoon table salt	2 extra-large eggs, cold
11 tablespoons (or ⅔ cup) unsalted butter, cold and cubed	1½ teaspoons pure vanilla extract
11 tablespoons (or ⅔ cup) vegetable shortening, room temperature	2 cups (16 ounces) semisweet chocolate chips

Preheat the oven to 350°F.

In a medium bowl, stir together the flour, baking soda, and salt. Set aside.

In a large mixing bowl or the bowl of a stand mixer, combine the butter, shortening, sugar, brown sugar, eggs, and vanilla extract and beat on medium-low speed until mixed with just small chunks of butter remaining, approximately 30 seconds. Every time you mix ingredients, scrape down the sides of the bowl with a spatula to be sure all ingredients are included in the mix—every bit matters! Add half of the dry ingredient mixture and mix on low speed until just incorporated and no flour is visible, about 30 seconds. Add half of the remaining dry ingredients and mix on low speed until the flour is incorporated and all butter chunks are gone, approximately 20 seconds. Add the remaining dry ingredients and mix until the dough pulls away from the sides of the bowl and is not sticky to the touch, about 20 seconds. Be careful not to overmix—that's how you get flat cookies. Stir in the chocolate chips.

Line two baking sheets with parchment paper. Scoop the dough ⅓ cup at a time and firmly roll into round balls approximately 1½ inches in diameter. Place 6 cookies on each prepared baking sheet, spacing them out well. Bake on the middle and lower racks of the oven until the tops are a light golden brown and you notice hairline cracks forming on the sides, 12 to 14 minutes, spinning each pan 180 degrees and swapping their positions halfway through.

Let the cookies cool on the baking sheets for 10 minutes, then use a wide spatula to transfer them to a wire rack or parchment paper on the counter to cool completely. Let the baking sheets cool before repeating with the remaining cookies.

Store in an airtight container at room temperature for up to 4 days or freeze for up to a month.

---

* **NOTE:** If you're living a life free from gluten, this is an easy recipe to make gluten free! Simply substitute the all-purpose flour with 4 cups plus 2 tablespoons of gluten-free baking flour (I prefer Cup4Cup brand) and reduce the chocolate chips to 1¾ cups. One trick to get the gluten-free version to bake perfectly is to mix the dough about 20 seconds longer when you add in the last of the flour mixture.

Scan for Tunes!

WHITE CHOCOLATE RASPBERRY COOKIES

I got my first job at age sixteen at Arlene's Corner Sweet Shoppe, a tiny specialty candy store in the local mall. We sold all kinds of treats from fudge to popcorn and Icees to fancy truffles and lottery tickets, and I loved it. I ran the place most days and even then, the experience of serving a customer something that made them a little happier lit me up inside. I also realized the impact a little shop can have on the community. I still think about the mall's custodians, Chris and Darlene, a married couple who stopped by daily for their Icees and lottery tickets. The first time I saw white chocolate and raspberry combined in a treat was while working there. It was in the form of a truffle then, but the combination never left my head, and I eventually created this cookie. I recommend buying fresh raspberries and freezing them; working with frozen berries will keep them from getting squishy and make your life a little easier. The sweet and tart flavors make this delightful treat a staff and fan favorite, and these cookies are sure to classy up any occasion!

Makes 15 to 18 three-inch cookies

4 cups all-purpose flour

1 teaspoon baking soda

1 teaspoon table salt

11 tablespoons (or ⅔ cup) unsalted butter, cold and cubed

11 tablespoons (or ⅔ cup) vegetable shortening, room temperature

1 cup sugar

1 cup packed light brown sugar

2 extra-large eggs, cold

1½ teaspoons pure vanilla extract

1¾ cups (14 ounces) white chocolate chips

2 cups fresh raspberries, frozen

Preheat the oven to 350°F.

In a medium bowl, stir together the flour, baking soda, and salt. Set aside.

In a large mixing bowl or the bowl of a stand mixer, combine the butter, shortening, sugar, brown sugar, eggs, and vanilla extract and beat on medium-low speed until mixed with just small chunks of butter remaining, approximately 30 seconds. Every time you mix ingredients, scrape down the sides of the bowl with a spatula to be sure all ingredients are included in the mix—every bit matters! Add half of the dry ingredient mixture and mix on low speed until just incorporated and no flour is visible, about 30 seconds. Add half of the remaining dry ingredients and mix on low speed until the flour is incorporated and all butter chunks are gone, approximately 20 seconds. Add the remaining dry ingredients and mix until the dough pulls away from the sides of the bowl and is not sticky to the touch, about 20 seconds. Be careful not to overmix—that's how you get flat cookies. Stir in the white chocolate chips.

Line two baking sheets with parchment paper. Scoop the dough ⅓ cup at a time and place a frozen raspberry in the middle of each scoop, making sure the berry is fully encased in dough. Firmly roll into round balls approximately 1½ inches in diameter. Place 6 cookies on each prepared baking sheet, spacing them out well. Top each cookie with half a frozen raspberry and bake on the middle and lower racks of the oven until the tops are a light golden brown and you notice hairline cracks forming on the sides, 12 to 14 minutes, spinning each pan 180 degrees and swapping their positions halfway through.

Let the cookies cool on the baking sheets for 10 minutes, then use a wide spatula to transfer them to a wire rack or parchment paper on the counter to cool completely. Let the baking sheets cool before repeating with the remaining cookies.

Store in an airtight container at room temperature for up to 3 days or freeze for up to a month.

---

* **NOTE:** Science is cool! In the hours and days after you bake these cookies, you might notice the insides turning a bit blue. This is caused by a reaction between the raspberry juice and baking soda and is not mold. However, given that these beauties contain fresh fruit, I definitely recommend freezing the cookies if you plan to eat them over more than a couple of days.

Scan for Video!

CHOCOLATE CHIP WALNUT COOKIES

Feeling nutty? Whip up a batch of what *might* be one of my favorite cookie flavors! While it took me a while to try the addition of walnuts because I just loved my chocolate chip cookies so much, I have since seen the error of my ways. There is something magical about the way the walnuts interact with the dough and the chocolate. The subtle texture they add and the way the walnut oil elevates the flavor of the dough is a sensory experience that's hard to beat. While you can certainly add any nut of your choosing, it's my humble opinion as a flavor matchmaker that the chocolate chip and walnut are made for each other.

Makes 15 to 18 three-inch cookies

¾ cup chopped walnut pieces

4 cups all-purpose flour

1 teaspoon baking soda

1 teaspoon table salt

11 tablespoons (or ⅔ cup) unsalted butter, cold and cubed

11 tablespoons (or ⅔ cup) vegetable shortening, room temperature

1 cup sugar

1 cup packed light brown sugar

2 extra-large eggs, cold

1½ teaspoons pure vanilla extract

1½ cups (12 ounces) semisweet chocolate chips

Preheat the oven to 350°F.

Using a knife, finely chop the walnut pieces. I have found that chopping them into smaller pieces releases their delicious oil and also guarantees that you get walnut bits in every bite.

In a medium bowl, stir together the flour, baking soda, and salt. Set aside.

In a large mixing bowl or the bowl of a stand mixer, combine the butter, shortening, sugar, brown sugar, eggs, and vanilla extract and beat on medium-low speed until mixed with just small chunks of butter remaining, approximately 30 seconds. Every time you mix ingredients, scrape down the sides of the bowl with a spatula to be sure all ingredients are included in the mix—every bit matters! Add half of the dry ingredient mixture and mix on low speed until just incorporated and no flour is visible, about 30 seconds. Add half of the remaining dry ingredients and mix on low speed until the flour is incorporated and all butter chunks are gone, approximately 20 seconds. Add the remaining dry ingredients and mix until the dough pulls away from the sides of the bowl and is not sticky to the touch, about 20 seconds. Be careful not to overmix—that's how you get flat cookies. Stir in the chocolate chips and walnuts.

Line two baking sheets with parchment paper. Scoop the dough ⅓ cup at a time and firmly roll into round balls approximately 1½ inches in diameter. Place 6 cookies on each prepared baking sheet, spacing them out well. Bake on the middle and lower racks of the oven until the tops are a light golden brown and you notice hairline cracks forming on the sides, 12 to 14 minutes, spinning each pan 180 degrees and swapping their positions halfway through.

Let the cookies cool on the baking sheets for 10 minutes, then use a wide spatula to transfer them to a wire rack or parchment paper on the counter to cool completely. Let the baking sheets cool before repeating with the remaining cookies.

Store in an airtight container at room temperature for up to 4 days or freeze for up to a month.

CHOCOLATE CHOCOLATE CHIP COOKIES

This cookie, while simple, is a little piece of chocolate heaven. As a chocolate lover, I truly never tire of this cookie. When I was developing this recipe, I wanted to achieve a rich, chocolatey flavor without compromising the signature texture that make my cookies special. By slightly decreasing the amount of flour to make room for the cocoa powder, I got the perfect result. This also became the base for a couple of other delightful flavors. Swap out the chocolate chips for white chocolate chips to experience the Inside-Out Chocolate Chip Cookie, which is reminiscent of a chocolate toaster pastry. Yum! Or follow the dough rolling method used in the White Chocolate Raspberry Cookie recipe on page 17, and add the raspberries as described to create my brother's favorite—Chocolate Raspberry Cookies . I personally live by the motto "not either/or, but both and more" and make a little of each!

Makes 15 to 18 three-inch cookies

3½ cups all-purpose flour	1 cup sugar
⅓ cup natural unsweetened cocoa powder	1 cup packed light brown sugar
1 teaspoon baking soda	2 extra-large eggs, cold
1 teaspoon table salt	1½ teaspoons pure vanilla extract
11 tablespoons (or ⅔ cup) unsalted butter, cold and cubed	2 cups (16 ounces) semisweet chocolate chips
11 tablespoons (or ⅔ cup) vegetable shortening, room temperature	

Preheat the oven to 350°F.

In a medium bowl, stir together the flour, cocoa powder, baking soda, and salt. Set aside.

In a large mixing bowl or the bowl of a stand mixer, combine the butter, shortening, sugar, brown sugar, eggs, and vanilla extract and beat on medium-low speed until mixed with just small chunks of butter remaining, approximately 30 seconds. Every time you mix ingredients, scrape down the sides of the bowl with a spatula to be sure all ingredients are included in the mix—every bit matters! Add half of the dry ingredient mixture and mix on low speed until just incorporated and no flour is visible, about 30 seconds. Add half of the remaining dry ingredients and mix on low speed until the flour is incorporated and all butter chunks are gone, approximately 20 seconds. Add the remaining dry ingredients and mix until the dough pulls away from the sides of the bowl and is not sticky to the touch, about 20 seconds. Be careful not to overmix—that's how you get flat cookies. Stir in the chocolate chips.

Line two baking sheets with parchment paper. Scoop the dough ⅓ cup at a time and firmly roll into round balls approximately 1½ inches in diameter. Place 6 cookies on each prepared baking sheet, spacing them out well. Bake on the middle and lower racks of the oven until the tops are a light golden brown and you notice hairline cracks forming on the sides, 12 to 14 minutes, spinning each pan 180 degrees and swapping their positions halfway through.

Let the cookies cool on the baking sheets for 10 minutes, then use a wide spatula to transfer them to a wire rack or parchment paper on the counter to cool completely. Let the baking sheets cool before repeating with the remaining cookies.

Store in an airtight container at room temperature for up to 4 days or freeze for up to a month.

WHITE CHOCOLATE MACADAMIA COOKIES

Growing up, no trip to the mall was ever complete without a quick snack. No surprise, my go-to was often a cookie! I've always been a big fan of salty-sweet combos, so a natural choice would have been a white chocolate–macadamia cookie. Sadly, I was never satisfied with the available versions, so I took matters into my own hands. I found the key to this classic to be the delicate flavor balance between the sweet and salty, where they work together and one doesn't overpower the other. So, for the roasted macadamias, I use a mix of salted and unsalted. If you can only find salted macadamias, decrease the salt in the dough to ¾ teaspoon. Moral of the story: get yourself some plastic bags and make your mall outings BYOC.

Makes 15 to 18 three-inch cookies

½ cup roasted salted macadamia nuts, chopped

¼ cup roasted unsalted macadamia nuts, chopped

4 cups all-purpose flour

1 teaspoon baking soda

1 teaspoon table salt

11 tablespoons (or ⅔ cup) unsalted butter, cold and cubed

11 tablespoons (or ⅔ cup) vegetable shortening, room temperature

1 cup sugar

1 cup packed light brown sugar

2 extra-large eggs, cold

1½ teaspoons pure vanilla extract

1½ cups (12 ounces) white chocolate chips

Preheat the oven to 350°F.

Using a knife, finely chop the macadamia nuts into pieces. I have found that chopping them into smaller pieces releases their delicious oil and also guarantees that you get macadamia bits in every bite.

In a medium bowl, stir together the flour, baking soda, and salt. Set aside.

In a large mixing bowl or the bowl of a stand mixer, combine the butter, shortening, sugar, brown sugar, eggs, and vanilla extract and beat on medium-low speed until mixed with just small chunks of butter remaining, approximately 30 seconds. Every time you mix ingredients, scrape down the sides of the bowl with a spatula to be sure all ingredients are included in the mix—every bit matters! Add half of the dry ingredient mixture and mix on low speed until just incorporated and no flour is visible, about 30 seconds. Add half of the remaining dry ingredients and mix on low speed until the flour is incorporated and all butter chunks are gone, approximately 20 seconds. Add the remaining dry ingredients and mix until the dough pulls away from the sides of the bowl and is not sticky to the touch, about 20 seconds. Be careful not to overmix—that's how you get flat cookies. Stir in the white chocolate chips and macadamia nuts.

Line two baking sheets with parchment paper. Scoop the dough ⅓ cup at a time and firmly roll into round balls approximately 1½ inches in diameter. Place 6 cookies on each prepared baking sheet, spacing them out well. Bake on the middle and lower racks of the oven until the tops are a light golden brown and you notice hairline cracks forming on the sides, 12 to 14 minutes, spinning each pan 180 degrees and swapping their positions halfway through.

Let the cookies cool on the baking sheets for 10 minutes, then use a wide spatula to transfer them to a wire rack or parchment paper on the counter to cool completely. Let the baking sheets cool before repeating with the remaining cookies.

Store in an airtight container at room temperature for up to 4 days or freeze for up to a month.

BANANA SPLIT COOKIES

Coming up with new cookie flavors is such a fun, creative outlet. One period of experimentation found me inspired by ice cream, and 1 of course considered the banana split. *Hmmm . . . could 1 make that into a cookie?* 1 was sure going to try. So, 1 started playing around and was convinced of one thing: it was going to be really delicious or really bad! Thankfully, it was the former and has since become Milk Jar's second-best seller and quite the press darling. Local publications caught wind of this cookie immediately upon opening our doors, and the fascination continues, including a recent segment on the Cooking Channel show *The Best Thing 1 Ever Ate*, proving that while everyone loves a classic, they clearly crave adventure and creativity, too! One tip when you make this one: make sure you dry your strawberry slices very well before placing them in and on top of the dough balls to keep them from sliding around. For the full banana split experience, pair these with a scoop of vanilla ice cream, and heaven awaits.

Makes 15 to 18 three-inch cookies

10 fresh strawberries, quartered

¾ cup chopped walnut pieces

4 cups all-purpose flour

1 teaspoon baking soda

1 teaspoon table salt

11 tablespoons (or ⅔ cup) unsalted butter, cold and cubed

11 tablespoons (or ⅔ cup) vegetable shortening, room temperature

1 cup sugar

1 cup packed light brown sugar

2 extra-large eggs, cold

1½ teaspoons pure vanilla extract

1½ teaspoons pure banana extract

⅔ cup (5 ounces) semisweet chocolate chips

⅔ cup (5 ounces) butterscotch chips

Preheat the oven to 350°F.

Wash the strawberries and dry thoroughly with a paper towel. Quarter each strawberry and place on a plate or tray lined with paper towels to absorb excess juice. Set aside.

Using a knife, finely chop the walnuts into pieces. I have found that chopping them into smaller pieces releases their delicious oil and also guarantees that you get walnut bits in every bite. Set aside.

In a medium bowl, stir together the flour, baking soda, and salt. Set aside.

In a large mixing bowl or the bowl of a stand mixer, combine the butter, shortening, sugar, brown sugar, eggs, vanilla extract, and banana extract and beat on medium-low speed until mixed with just small chunks of butter remaining, approximately 30 seconds. Every time you mix ingredients, scrape down the sides of the bowl with a spatula to be sure all ingredients are included in the mix—every bit matters! Add half of the dry ingredient mixture and mix on low speed until just incorporated and no flour is visible, about 30 seconds. Add half of the remaining dry ingredients and mix on low speed until the flour is incorporated and all butter chunks are gone, approximately 20 seconds. Add the remaining dry ingredients and mix until the dough pulls away from the sides of the bowl and is not sticky to the touch, about 20 seconds. Be careful not to overmix—that's how you get flat cookies. Stir in the chocolate chips, butterscotch chips, and walnuts.

Line two baking sheets with parchment paper. Scoop the dough ⅓ cup at a time and place a strawberry slice in the middle of each scoop, making sure the berry is fully encased in dough. Firmly roll into round balls approximately 1½ inches in diameter. While the dough ball is still in your hands, top each cookie with a strawberry slice, gently pushing it in to keep it in position while they bake. Place 6 cookies on each prepared baking sheet, spacing them out well. Bake on the middle and lower racks of the oven until the tops are a light golden brown and you notice hairline cracks forming on the sides, 12 to 14 minutes, spinning each pan 180 degrees and swapping their positions halfway through.

Let the cookies cool on the baking sheets for 10 minutes, then use a wide spatula to transfer them to a wire rack or parchment paper on the counter to cool completely. Let the baking sheets cool before repeating with the remaining cookies.

Store in an airtight container at room temperature for up to 4 days or freeze for up to a month.

CINNAMON SUGAR COOKIES

Sometimes all you need is the flavor of butter, sugar, and a little cinnamon for a sublime treat. In my opinion, this simple cookie is perfection. Some might call this a snickerdoodle, but I like to call out the real stars: cinnamon and sugar. My mom's cinnamon sugar mixture that she, to this day, keeps in her light blue Tupperware container, was the inspiration for this cookie. A go-to breakfast growing up was a piece of cinnamon toast and a glass of chocolate milk (mom jokes now that she was a terrible mother sending us off to school with that in our bellies, but we definitely disagree— she's the best). I highly recommend starting your own container of it to have on hand to sprinkle on a piece of buttered toast if you don't have time to make a whole batch of cookies. But, either way, cookie or toast, don't forget the chocolate milk!

Makes 15 to 18 three-inch cookies

FOR THE TOPPING:

1 cup sugar

1 tablespoon ground cinnamon

FOR THE COOKIES:

4 cups all-purpose flour

1 teaspoon baking soda

1 teaspoon table salt

11 tablespoons (or ⅔ cup) unsalted butter, cold and cubed

11 tablespoons (or ⅔ cup) vegetable shortening, room temperature

1 cup sugar

1 cup packed light brown sugar

2 extra-large eggs, cold

1½ teaspoons pure vanilla extract

TO MAKE THE TOPPING: In a small bowl, stir together the sugar and cinnamon until thoroughly combined. This mixture can be made in advance and stored in an airtight container for several months. If you want to make more to keep on hand and use on other treats, just keep the ratio 1:1.

TO MAKE THE COOKIES: Preheat oven to 350°F.

In a medium bowl, stir together the flour, baking soda, and salt. Set aside.

In a large mixing bowl or the bowl of a stand mixer, combine the butter, shortening, sugar, brown sugar, eggs, and vanilla extract and beat on medium-low speed until mixed with just small chunks of butter remaining, approximately 30 seconds. Every time you mix ingredients, scrape down the sides of the bowl with a spatula to be sure all ingredients are included in the mix—every bit matters! Add half of the dry ingredient mixture and mix on low speed until just incorporated and no flour is visible, about 30 seconds. Add half of the remaining dry ingredients and mix on low speed until the flour is incorporated and all butter chunks are gone, approximately 20 seconds. Add the remaining dry ingredients and mix until the dough pulls away from the sides of the bowl and is not sticky to the touch, about 20 seconds. Be careful not to overmix—that's how you get flat cookies.

Line two baking sheets with parchment paper. Scoop the dough ¼ cup at a time and firmly roll into round balls each approximately 1 inch in diameter. Before placing 6 cookies on each prepared baking sheet, roll the top of each dough ball in your cinnamon sugar mixture. The secret to a fully covered cookie is to make sure your bowl of cinnamon sugar is deeper than it is wide, allowing the top half of the dough ball to be immersed in the mixture. Bake on the middle and lower racks of the oven until the tops are a light golden brown and you notice hairline cracks forming on the sides, 11 to 13 minutes, spinning each pan 180 degrees and swapping their positions halfway through.

Let the cookies cool on the baking sheets for 10 minutes, then use a wide spatula to transfer them to a wire rack or parchment paper on the counter to cool completely. Let the baking sheets cool before repeating with the remaining cookies.

Store in an airtight container at room temperature for up to 4 days or freeze for up to a month.

→ **RECIPE ALTERNATIVE:** Birthday Cookies! Simply substitute the cinnamon sugar topping with rainbow nonpareils. Not only do they add the perfect pop of color to any celebration (or just any day), but the crunchy texture the nonpareils add to each bite makes this one of Milk Jar's best-selling cookies. While these two cookies are Milk Jar staples, the dough itself is an amazing, delicious canvas, so let your creativity run wild! Brown sugar and cardamom? Sure! Orange zest? Why not?!

Scan for Video!

ROCKY ROAD COOKIES

Rocky road is one of my favorite ice cream flavors, and I knew I had to pay homage to it in my medium. I truly couldn't love this cookie more. The textures are such a delight, the way the marshmallow gets a little crispy on top but is all ooey gooey inside the chocolate cookie, and the crunch of the almonds balances it all out . . . exquisite. I recommend eating these cookies warm, and don't cheat yourself out of the experience of enjoying them with an ice-cold glass of milk.

Makes 15 to 18 three-inch cookies

3½ cups all-purpose flour	1 cup packed light brown sugar
⅓ cup natural unsweetened cocoa powder	2 extra-large eggs, cold
1 teaspoon baking soda	1½ teaspoons pure vanilla extract
1 teaspoon table salt	1½ cups (12 ounces) semisweet chocolate chips
11 tablespoons (or ⅔ cup) unsalted butter, cold and cubed	¾ cup slivered almonds
11 tablespoons (or ⅔ cup) vegetable shortening, room temperature	Mini marshmallows (4 per cookie, approximately 72)
1 cup sugar	

Preheat the oven to 350°F.

In a medium bowl, stir together the flour, cocoa powder, baking soda, and salt. Set aside.

In a large mixing bowl or the bowl of a stand mixer, combine the butter, shortening, sugar, brown sugar, eggs, and vanilla extract and beat on medium-low speed until mixed with just small chunks of butter remaining, approximately 30 seconds. Every time you mix ingredients, scrape down the sides of the bowl with a spatula to be sure all ingredients are included in the mix—every bit matters! Add half of the dry ingredient mixture and mix on low speed until just incorporated and no flour is visible, about 30 seconds. Add half of the remaining dry ingredients and mix on low speed until the flour is incorporated and all butter chunks are gone, approximately 20 seconds. Add the

remaining dry ingredients and mix until the dough pulls away from the sides of the bowl and is not sticky to the touch, about 20 seconds. Be careful not to overmix—that's how you get flat cookies. Stir in the chocolate chips and almonds.

Line two baking sheets with parchment paper. Scoop the dough ⅓ cup at a time and place 2 mini marshmallows in the middle of each scoop, making sure they are fully encased in dough. Firmly roll into round balls approximately 1½ inches in diameter. While the dough ball is still in your hands, top each cookie with 2 more marshmallows, gently pushing them in to keep them in position while they bake. Place 6 cookies on each prepared baking sheet, spacing them out well. Bake on the middle and upper racks of the oven until the marshmallows on top are a light golden brown and you notice hairline cracks forming on the sides, 12 to 14 minutes, spinning each pan 180 degrees and swapping their positions halfway through.

Let the cookies cool on the baking sheets for 10 minutes, then use a wide spatula to transfer them to a wire rack or parchment paper on the counter to cool completely. Let the baking sheets cool before repeating with the remaining cookies.

Store in an airtight container at room temperature for up to 4 days or freeze for up to a month.

OATMEAL RAISIN COOKIES

While my dad has never met a sweet he doesn't like, he's always had a special place in his heart for an oatmeal raisin cookie. When I was developing my recipes, it was a given that I had to create my take on this classic, and it had to be good enough to elicit my dad's signature giddy "ooooooh" wiggle dance. It does not disappoint (the cookie or his dance)! The smell of baked raisins and cinnamon wafting from the oven will set the stage, and the soft, chewy results are sure to make you dance with delight, too. For the juiciest results, use Sun-Maid raisins—they are shriveled to perfection. If you're not a fan of raisins, swap them out for chocolate chips. Oatmeal Chocolate Chip is a fan favorite at my shop and the cookie my husband craves regularly.

Makes 18 to 20 three-inch cookies

2 cups all-purpose flour	½ cup sugar
1 teaspoon baking powder	1 cup packed light brown sugar
¼ teaspoon baking soda	2 extra-large eggs, cold
½ teaspoon table salt	1½ teaspoons pure vanilla extract
½ heaping teaspoon ground cinnamon	3½ cups rolled oats (not instant oats)
4 tablespoons (or ¼ cup) unsalted butter, cold and cubed	1½ cups raisins
8 tablespoons (or ½ cup) vegetable shortening, room temperature	

Preheat the oven to 350°F.

In a medium bowl, stir together the flour, baking powder, baking soda, salt, and cinnamon. Set aside.

In a large mixing bowl or the bowl of a stand mixer, combine the butter, shortening, sugar, and brown sugar and beat on medium speed until creamed, approximately 1 minute. Scrape down the sides of the bowl with a spatula to be sure all ingredients are included in the mix—every bit matters! Add the eggs and vanilla extract and mix until combined and the mixture is smooth. Add the entire bowl of dry ingredients at once and mix on medium speed until it's fully combined and no flour is visible, about 1 minute. Scrape the sides of the bowl again. Add the oats and mix on low speed or stir by hand until just combined. Maintaining the integrity of the oats will help you get the perfect texture in your cookies. Stir in the raisins.

Line two baking sheets with parchment paper. Scoop the dough ¼ cup at a time and place 8 cookies on each prepared baking sheet, spacing them out well. Using your fingers, gently flatten each cookie until they look like flat haystacks. The cookies won't spread when you bake them, so you want to shape them into their final desired form at this point. Bake on the middle and lower racks of the oven until the edges are just golden brown and the centers of the cookies no longer look wet, 11 to 13 minutes, spinning each pan 180 degrees and swapping their positions halfway through.

Let the cookies cool on the baking sheet for 10 minutes, then use a wide spatula to transfer them to a wire rack to cool completely. Let the baking sheets cool before repeating with the remaining cookies.

Store in an airtight container at room temperature for up to 4 days or freeze for up to a month.

➡ RECIPE ALTERNATIVE: If you're looking for a pretty, festive dessert for a holiday gathering, try replacing the raisins with ¾ cup each dried cranberries and white chocolate chips. So many options!

Scan for Video!

CHOCOLATE PECAN CARAMEL COOKIES

When I was developing my initial recipes, I knew I wanted to do something with caramel. Chocolate-covered caramels and chocolate-caramel nut clusters have always been my favorite specialty candies, and I wanted a cookie version of that. Should I use caramel squares? Hard caramels? Caramel sauce? Rolos? Well, I tried them all and made my friend Sarah sick in the process, as she tasted each creation. Turns out that Rolos are clutch. They melt perfectly and complement the chocolate dough and pecan pieces to create a mouthwateringly decadent treat. Here's to you eating *just* the right amount!

Makes 15 to 18 three-inch cookies

3½ cups all-purpose flour	1 cup sugar
⅓ cup natural unsweetened cocoa powder	1 cup packed light brown sugar
1 teaspoon baking soda	2 extra-large eggs, cold
1 teaspoon table salt	1½ teaspoons pure vanilla extract
11 tablespoons (or ⅔ cup) unsalted butter, cold and cubed	1½ cups pecan pieces
11 tablespoons (or ⅔ cup) vegetable shortening, room temperature	Rolo candies, cut in half (4 halves per cookie, approximately 72)

Preheat the oven to 350°F.

In a medium bowl, stir together the flour, cocoa powder, baking soda, and salt. Set aside.

In a large mixing bowl or the bowl of a stand mixer, combine the butter, shortening, sugar, brown sugar, eggs, and vanilla extract and beat on medium-low speed until mixed with just small chunks of butter remaining, approximately 30 seconds. Every time you mix ingredients, scrape down the sides of the bowl with a spatula to be sure all ingredients are included in the mix—every bit matters! Add half of the dry ingredient mixture and mix on low speed until just incorporated and no flour is visible, about 30 seconds. Add half of the remaining dry ingredients and mix on low speed until the flour is incorporated and all butter chunks are gone, approximately 20 seconds. Add the remaining dry ingredients and mix until the dough pulls away from the sides of the bowl and is not sticky to the touch, about 20 seconds. Be careful not to overmix—that's how you get flat cookies. Stir in the pecans.

Line two baking sheets with parchment paper. Scoop the dough ⅓ cup at a time and place 2 Rolo halves in the middle of each scoop, making sure the candies are fully encased in dough. Firmly roll into round balls approximately 1½ inches in diameter. While the dough ball is still in your hands, top each cookie with 2 more Rolo halves, gently pushing them in to keep them in position while they bake. Place 6 cookies on each prepared baking sheet, spacing them out well. Bake on the middle and lower racks of the oven until the caramel candies are melted and you notice hairline cracks forming on the sides, 12 to 14 minutes, spinning each pan 180 degrees and swapping their positions halfway through.

Let the cookies cool on the baking sheets for 10 minutes, then use a wide spatula to transfer them to a wire rack or parchment paper on the counter to cool completely. Let the baking sheets cool before repeating with the remaining cookies.

Store in an airtight container at room temperature for up to 4 days or freeze for up to a month.

SALTED BUTTERSCOTCH COOKIES

After making homemade butterscotch pudding for a Milk Jar holiday party and getting rave reviews about it, I knew I had to develop a cookie with that flavor profile. The rich, sweet butterscotch combined with the crispy salt flakes made it an immediate fan-favorite seasonal flavor in the shop; barely a week passes without a customer asking when this cookie will be around again. Lucky you, you can have it anytime the craving hits! Note that there is a fine line between just salty enough and inedible, but if you accidentally oversalt your cookies, just scrape off some of the salt, to taste.

Makes 15 to 18 three-inch cookies

4 cups all-purpose flour

1 teaspoon baking soda

1 teaspoon table salt

11 tablespoons (or ⅔ cup) unsalted butter, cold and cubed

11 tablespoons (or ⅔ cup) vegetable shortening, room temperature

1 cup sugar

1 cup packed light brown sugar

2 extra-large eggs, cold

1½ teaspoons pure vanilla extract

2 cups (16 ounces) butterscotch chips

Maldon sea salt flakes, for sprinkling

Preheat the oven to 350°F.

In a medium bowl, stir together the flour, baking soda, and salt. Set aside.

In a large mixing bowl or the bowl of a stand mixer, combine the butter, shortening, sugar, brown sugar, eggs, and vanilla extract and beat on medium-low speed until mixed with just small chunks of butter remaining, approximately 30 seconds. Every time you mix ingredients, scrape down the sides of the bowl with a spatula to be sure all ingredients are included in the mix—every bit matters! Add half of the dry ingredient mixture and mix on low speed until just incorporated and no flour is visible, about 30 seconds. Add half of the remaining dry ingredients and mix on low speed until the flour is incorporated and all butter chunks are gone, approximately 20 seconds. Add the

remaining dry ingredients and mix until the dough pulls away from the sides of the bowl and is not sticky to the touch, about 20 seconds. Be careful not to overmix—that's how you get flat cookies. Stir in the butterscotch chips.

Line two baking sheets with parchment paper. Scoop the dough ⅓ cup at a time and firmly roll into round balls approximately 1½ inches in diameter. Place 6 cookies on each prepared baking sheet, spacing them out well. Bake on the middle and lower racks of the oven until the tops are a light golden brown and you notice hairline cracks forming on the sides, 12 to 14 minutes, spinning each pan 180 degrees and swapping their positions halfway through. As soon as you take the cookies out of the oven, sprinkle the top of each cookie with salt flakes, to taste.

Let the cookies cool on the baking sheets for 10 minutes, then use a wide spatula to transfer them to a wire rack or parchment paper on the counter to cool completely. Let the baking sheets cool before repeating with the remaining cookies.

Store in an airtight container at room temperature for up to 4 days or freeze for up to a month.

➡ **RECIPE ALTERNATIVE:** If you're living a life free from gluten, this is an easy recipe to make gluten free! Simply substitute the all-purpose flour with 4 cups plus 2 tablespoons of gluten-free baking flour (I prefer Cup4Cup brand) and reduce the butterscotch chips to 1¾ cups. One trick to get the gluten-free version to bake perfectly is to mix the dough about 20 seconds longer when you add in the last of the flour mixture.

MINT CHOCOLATE COOKIES

As a lifelong Girl Scout (top-selling cookie member of my troop on a couple of occasions, thank you very much), I have quite the affinity for a Thin Mint. In fact, it's the only hard cookie I enjoy. So, I of course had to develop my soft, gooey take on it. The rich, chocolatey dough and the melted Andes mints create a flavor you may well climb a mountain for. I've learned from customers that the combination of mint and chocolate is a controversial topic, so if you're on the opposing team, slowly back away. However, if you're a fan, this may well become your favorite recipe in this book.

Makes 15 to 18 three-inch cookies

3½ cups all-purpose flour	1 cup sugar
⅓ cup natural unsweetened cocoa powder	1 cup packed light brown sugar
1 teaspoon baking soda	2 extra-large eggs, cold
1 teaspoon table salt	1½ teaspoons pure vanilla extract
11 tablespoons (or ⅔ cup) unsalted butter, cold and cubed	1½ teaspoons pure peppermint extract
11 tablespoons (or ⅔ cup) vegetable shortening, room temperature	1¾ cups (14 ounces) Andes Crème de Menthe Thin Mints, coarsely chopped

Preheat the oven to 350°F.

In a medium bowl, stir together the flour, cocoa powder, baking soda, and salt. Set aside.

In a large mixing bowl or the bowl of a stand mixer, combine the butter, shortening, sugar, brown sugar, eggs, vanilla extract, and peppermint extract and beat on medium-low speed until mixed with just small chunks of butter remaining, approximately 30 seconds. Every time you mix ingredients, scrape down the sides of the bowl with a spatula to be sure all ingredients are included in the mix—every bit matters! Add half of the dry ingredient mixture and mix on low speed until just incorporated and no flour is visible, about 30 seconds. Add half of the remaining dry ingredients and mix on low speed until the flour is incorporated and all butter chunks are gone, approximately

20 seconds. Add the remaining dry ingredients and mix until the dough pulls away from the sides of the bowl and is not sticky to the touch, about 20 seconds. Be careful not to overmix—that's how you get flat cookies. Stir in the mints.

Line two baking sheets with parchment paper. Scoop the dough ⅓ cup at a time and firmly roll into round balls approximately 1½ inches in diameter. Place 6 cookies on each prepared baking sheet, spacing them out well. Bake on the middle and lower racks of the oven until the tops are a light golden brown and you notice hairline cracks forming on the sides, 12 to 14 minutes, spinning each pan 180 degrees and swapping their positions halfway through.

Let the cookies cool on the baking sheets for 10 minutes, then use a wide spatula to transfer them to a wire rack or parchment paper on the counter to cool completely. Let the baking sheets cool before repeating with the remaining cookies.

Store in an airtight container at room temperature for up to 4 days or freeze for up to a month.

KEY LIME PIE COOKIES

❦

This tart little delight is the perfect way to welcome summer or brighten up a dreary winter day. I created this cookie for my sister's wedding, to celebrate her husband's childhood in the Florida Keys. The *ahem* marriage of flavors and textures in this cookie are so fun and keep your taste buds intrigued. Creamy white chocolate accented by that bright Key lime flavor and punctuated by the crunch of the pistachios—wedded bliss indeed.

Makes 15 to 18 three-inch cookies

1 cup roasted pistachio nuts, chopped

4 cups all-purpose flour

1 teaspoon baking soda

1 teaspoon table salt

11 tablespoons (or ⅔ cup) unsalted butter, cold and cubed

11 tablespoons (or ⅔ cup) vegetable shortening, room temperature

1 cup sugar

1 cup packed light brown sugar

2 extra-large eggs, cold

1½ teaspoons pure vanilla extract

1½ teaspoons pure Key lime extract

1½ cups (12 ounces) white chocolate chips

½ cup coarse sugar for topping

Preheat the oven to 350°F.

Using a knife, finely chop the pistachio nuts into pieces and set them aside. I have found that chopping them into smaller pieces releases their delicious oil and also guarantees that you get pistachio bits in every bite.

In a medium bowl, stir together the flour, baking soda, and salt. Set aside.

In a large mixing bowl or the bowl of a stand mixer, combine the butter, shortening, sugar, brown sugar, eggs, vanilla extract, and Key lime extract and beat on medium-low speed until mixed with just small chunks of butter remaining, approximately 30 seconds. Every time you mix ingredients, scrape down the sides of the bowl with a spatula to be sure all ingredients are included in the mix—every bit matters! Add half of the dry ingredient mixture and mix on low speed until just incorporated and no flour is visible, about 30 seconds. Add half of the remaining dry ingredients and mix on low speed until the flour is incorporated and all butter chunks are gone, approximately 20 seconds. Add the remaining dry ingredients and mix until the dough pulls away from the sides of the bowl and is not sticky to the touch, about 20 seconds. Be careful not to overmix—that's how you get flat cookies. Stir in the white chocolate chips and pistachio nuts.

Line two baking sheets with parchment paper. Scoop the dough ⅓ cup at a time and firmly roll into round balls approximately 1 inch in diameter. Roll the top of each dough ball in a small bowl of coarse sugar before placing 6 cookies on each prepared baking sheet, sugar side up. Bake on the middle and lower racks of the oven until the tops are a light golden brown and you notice hairline cracks forming on the sides, 12 to 14 minutes, spinning each pan 180 degrees and swapping their positions halfway through.

Let the cookies cool on the baking sheets for 10 minutes, then use a wide spatula to transfer them to a wire rack or parchment paper on the counter to cool completely. Let the baking sheets cool before repeating with the remaining cookies.

Store in an airtight container at room temperature for up to 4 days or freeze for up to a month.

Scan for Tunes!

WAFFLE COOKIES

I gain inspiration for new cookie flavors everywhere. This one was inspired by the TV show *Stranger Things* and the character Eleven's affinity for Eggo waffles. I created a "binge box" for my friends and family to enjoy as they binge-watched the new season. This cookie was so well received that I brought it out at the shop as a seasonal flavor. You might say that on a scale of 1 to 10, this cookie goes to 11. *wink*

Makes 15 to 18 three-inch cookies

5 toaster waffles, preferably Eggo, of course!

4 cups all-purpose flour

1 teaspoon baking soda

1 teaspoon table salt

11 tablespoons (or ⅔ cup) unsalted butter, cold and cubed

11 tablespoons (or ⅔ cup) vegetable shortening, room temperature

1 cup sugar

1 cup packed light brown sugar

2 extra-large eggs, cold

1½ teaspoons pure vanilla extract

1½ teaspoons pure maple extract

Preheat the oven to 350°F.

Toast the waffles to a golden brown according to package instructions and allow them to cool. Using kitchen scissors, cut 4 square pieces from the center of each waffle to create 4 mini waffles, as shown in the photo. Cut the leftover scraps into smaller pieces. The 4 square mini waffles will each become the tops of a cookie, while the smaller pieces will get mixed into the dough. Set aside.

In a medium bowl, stir together the flour, baking soda, and salt. Set aside.

In a large mixing bowl or the bowl of a stand mixer, combine the butter, shortening, sugar, brown sugar, eggs, vanilla extract, and maple extract and beat on medium-low speed until mixed with just small chunks of butter remaining, approximately 30 seconds. Every time you mix ingredients, scrape down the sides of the bowl with a spatula to be sure all ingredients are included in the mix—every bit matters! Add half of the dry ingredient mixture and mix on low speed until just incorporated and no flour is visible, about 30 seconds. Add half of the remaining dry ingredients and mix on low speed until the flour is incorporated and all butter chunks are gone, approximately 20 seconds. Add the remaining dry ingredients and mix until the dough pulls away from the sides of the bowl and is not sticky to the touch, about 20 seconds. Be careful not to overmix—that's how you get flat cookies. Stir in the small waffle pieces.

Line two baking sheets with parchment paper. Scoop the dough ⅓ cup at a time and firmly roll into round balls approximately 1½ inches in diameter. With the dough ball still in your hands, top each cookie with a mini waffle, gently pushing it in to keep it in position while they bake. (You will have extra mini waffles.) Place 6 cookies on each prepared baking sheet, spacing them out well. Bake on the middle and lower racks of the oven until the tops are a light golden brown and you notice hairline cracks forming on the sides, 12 to 14 minutes, spinning each pan 180 degrees and swapping their positions halfway through.

Let the cookies cool on the baking sheets for 10 minutes, then use a wide spatula to transfer them to a wire rack or parchment paper on the counter to cool completely. Let the baking sheets cool before repeating with the remaining cookies.

Store in an airtight container at room temperature for up to 4 days or freeze for up to a month.

PUMPKIN PIE COOKIES

My favorite time of year at Milk Jar Cookies is the holiday season. For a company built on spreading joy and love, this is our time to shine. The pinwheels hanging in the window turn to falling leaves and pumpkins, the air gets a little crisper, and the smell of nutmeg and cinnamon wafts through the shop as we kick off the season with my cookie incarnation of the quintessential Thanksgiving dessert. The palpably magical energy the fragrance creates is something special, and I can't wait for you to wrap yourselves up in this sensory hug.

P.S. The candied pecan topping is pure goodness and key to this cookie, and might I also suggest using some of the leftovers on a scoop of ice cream? Mmmmm . . . !

Makes 18 to 22 three-inch cookies

FOR THE CANDIED PECAN TOPPING:

4 cups pecan halves

1 tablespoon plus 1 teaspoon vegetable oil

¼ cup sugar

1 teaspoon ground cinnamon

1 teaspoon pumpkin pie spice

FOR THE COOKIES:

5½ cups all-purpose flour

2 teaspoons baking soda

1 teaspoon table salt

1 tablespoon plus 1 teaspoon pumpkin pie spice

1 teaspoon ground cinnamon

½ teaspoon ground nutmeg

11 tablespoons (or ⅔ cup) unsalted butter, cold and cubed

11 tablespoons (or ⅔ cup) vegetable shortening, room temperature

1 cup sugar

1 cup packed light brown sugar

2 extra-large eggs, cold

1½ teaspoons pure vanilla extract

1 cup 100 percent pure pumpkin puree

TO MAKE THE TOPPING: Preheat the oven to 375°F.

Using a knife, chop the pecan halves into pieces and transfer them to a medium bowl. Add the vegetable oil and toss to coat. Add the sugar, cinnamon, and pumpkin pie spice and toss until the nuts are evenly coated in spice mixture.

Line a baking sheet with parchment paper and spread the spiced pecans evenly across the pan. Bake for 10 minutes, rearranging them on the baking sheet halfway through for even toasting. Transfer back to the bowl and set aside. This topping can be made ahead of time and stored in an airtight container for up to 2 weeks.

TO MAKE THE COOKIES: Preheat the oven to 350°F.

In a medium bowl, stir together the flour, baking soda, salt, pumpkin pie spice, cinnamon, and nutmeg. Set aside.

In a large mixing bowl or the bowl of a stand mixer, combine the butter, shortening, sugar, brown sugar, eggs, and vanilla extract and beat on medium-low speed until mixed with just small chunks of butter remaining, approximately 30 seconds. Mix in the pumpkin puree until just combined. Every time you mix ingredients, scrape down the sides of the bowl with a spatula to be sure all ingredients are included in the mix—every bit matters! Add half of the dry ingredient mixture and mix on medium-low speed until just incorporated and no flour is visible, about 20 seconds. Add half of the remaining dry ingredients, mixing until no flour is visible and all the butter chunks are gone, about 20 seconds. Add the remaining dry ingredients and mix until no flour is visible and the dough is not sticky to the touch, about 30 more seconds.

Line two baking sheets with parchment paper. Scoop the dough ⅓ cup at a time and gently roll into round balls approximately 1½ inches in diameter. Press the top of each cookie into the bowl of candied pecans, coating the top, then place up to 8 cookies (pecan side up) on each prepared baking sheet, spacing them out well, and press the topping in to secure it. Note that the dough will be soft and the balls will softly flatten into discs approximately 2½ inches in diameter during this process. Bake on the middle and lower racks of the oven until the bottom edges are a deep orange and the centers no longer appear wet, yet are still dewy, 12 to 14 minutes, spinning each pan 180 degrees and swapping their positions halfway through.

Let the cookies cool on the baking sheet for 10 minutes, then use a wide spatula to transfer them to a wire rack to cool completely. Let the baking sheets cool before repeating with the remaining cookies.

Store in an airtight container at room temperature for up to 4 days or freeze for up to a month.

CHOCOLATE-COVERED BANANA COOKIES

Growing up, no summer was complete without a family trip to the "LDQ" (dad's nickname for the local Dairy Queen), and at least one of us would get a chocolate-covered banana. Color me happy when I moved to Los Angeles and could find them at every beachside snack stand! Spoiler alert—I felt compelled to create a cookie version of this classic. Banana chocolate dough combined with banana and chocolate chips, topped with a chocolate drizzle and crushed peanuts? It's almost like the real thing! While it requires several extra steps to make, I promise it is well worth the work. I highly recommend freezing a handful, and when you're ready to indulge, let the cookie(s) sit at room temperature for about twenty minutes before you dig in—they'll be perfectly cold and chewy.

Makes 15 to 18 three-inch cookies

¾ cup dried banana chips, crushed, plus 15–18 whole chips for topping cookies

3½ cups all-purpose flour

⅓ cup natural unsweetened cocoa powder

1 teaspoon baking soda

1 teaspoon table salt

11 tablespoons (or ⅔ cup) unsalted butter, cold and cubed

11 tablespoons (or ⅔ cup) vegetable shortening, room temperature

1 cup sugar

1 cup packed light brown sugar

2 extra-large eggs, cold

1½ teaspoons pure vanilla extract

1½ teaspoons pure banana extract

2½ cups (20 ounces) semisweet chocolate chips

Crushed peanuts, optional

Preheat the oven to 350°F.

With your hands, roughly crush ¾ cup of the dried banana chips into a bowl. Set aside.

In a medium bowl, stir together the flour, cocoa powder, baking soda, and salt. Set aside.

In a large mixing bowl or the bowl of a stand mixer, combine the butter, shortening, sugar, brown sugar, eggs, vanilla extract, and banana extract and beat on medium-low speed until mixed with just small chunks of butter remaining, approximately 30 seconds. Every time you mix ingredients, scrape down the sides of the bowl with a spatula to be sure all ingredients are included in the mix—every bit matters! Add half of the dry ingredient mixture and mix on low speed until just incorporated and no flour is visible, about 30 seconds. Add half of the remaining dry ingredients and mix on low speed until the flour is incorporated and all butter chunks are gone, approximately 20 seconds. Add the remaining dry ingredients and mix until the dough pulls away from the sides of the bowl and is not sticky to the touch, about 20 seconds. Be careful not to overmix—that's how you get flat cookies. Stir in 1½ cups of the chocolate chips and the banana chips you crushed earlier.

Line two baking sheets with parchment paper. Scooping the dough ⅓ cup at a time, firmly roll into round balls approximately 1½ inches in diameter. With the dough ball still in your hands, top each cookie with 1 full banana chip, gently pushing it in to keep it in position while they bake. Place 6 cookies on each prepared baking sheet, spacing them out well. Bake on the middle and lower oven racks until you notice hairline cracks forming on the sides, 12 to 14 minutes, spinning each pan 180 degrees and swapping their positions halfway through.

Let the cookies cool on the baking sheets for 10 minutes, then use a wide spatula to transfer them to a wire rack or parchment paper on the counter to cool completely. Let the baking sheets cool before repeating with the remaining cookies.

When the cookies have cooled completely, it's time to drizzle and top them! In a small, microwave-safe bowl, melt the remaining 1 cup chocolate chips in 30-second increments, stirring between each increment. Once the chocolate is melted, transfer to a piping bag with a skinny tip attached. Alternately, transfer to a plastic storage bag, work all the chocolate into one corner, and snip the corner off. In a zigzag motion and working from one side of each cookie to the other, drizzle the tops with chocolate. Sprinkle the top of each cookie with crushed peanuts, if desired. To accelerate the hardening of the chocolate and really get that "chocolate-covered" sensation, place your cookies in the refrigerator for 5 minutes before serving.

Store in an airtight container at room temperature for up to 4 days or freeze for up to a month.

PEANUT BUTTER COOKIES

❦

There are a few cookie flavors that are just classics. Peanut butter cookies are, for me, one of them. I mean, is there anything better than peanut butter? I'm not sure there is. In any form, it's just delicious. I digress. The use of both crunchy and creamy peanut butter adds a little texture that I enjoy a lot, but if you don't have both, just use ⅔ cup of the one you have on hand.

 *Makes 15 to 18 three-inch cookies*

3 cups all-purpose flour	⅓ cup creamy peanut butter
½ teaspoon baking soda	⅓ cup crunchy peanut butter
½ teaspoon baking powder	1 cup sugar, plus more for topping
½ teaspoon table salt	
5½ tablespoons (or ⅓ cup) unsalted butter, cold and cubed	1 cup packed light brown sugar
	2 extra-large eggs, cold
5½ tablespoons (or ⅓ cup) vegetable shortening, room temperature	1½ teaspoons pure vanilla extract

Preheat the oven to 350°F.

In a medium bowl, stir together the flour, baking soda, baking powder, and salt. Set aside.

In a large mixing bowl or the bowl of a stand mixer, combine the butter, shortening, creamy and crunchy peanut butters, sugar, and brown sugar and beat on medium speed until creamed, approximately 1 minute. Every time you mix ingredients, scrape down the sides of the bowl with a spatula to be sure all ingredients are included in the mix—every bit matters! Add the eggs and vanilla extract and mix until combined and the mixture is smooth, about 30 seconds. Add half the bowl of dry ingredients and mix on medium speed until it's fully combined and no flour is visible, about 20 seconds. Add the remaining flour and mix until just combined, about 20 seconds.

Line two baking sheets with parchment paper. Scoop the dough ¼ cup at a time and lightly roll into round balls approximately 1½ inches in diameter. Roll the top of each dough ball in a bowl of sugar, coating the top. Place 6 cookies on each prepared baking sheet, spacing them out well, and using a fork, make a crisscross pattern on top of each. Bake on the middle and lower racks of the oven until the tops are a light golden brown and you notice hairline cracks forming on the sides, 11 to 13 minutes, spinning each pan 180 degrees and swapping their positions halfway through.

Let the cookies cool on the baking sheets for 10 minutes, then use a wide spatula to transfer them to a wire rack or parchment paper on the counter to cool completely. Let the baking sheets cool before repeating with the remaining cookies.

Store in an airtight container at room temperature for up to 4 days or freeze for up to a month.

PICNIC COOKIES

You know when you plan to have a picnic and you suddenly decide that it is absolutely necessary to bring every single food and snack you've ever enjoyed and end up with far too much food? No, just me? Well, that quintessential summer experience that I never seem to learn from, no matter how many times it happens, was the inspiration for this cookie! There's a lot going on in here, but it is such a fun one to eat and just so yummy. And these make your next picnic a lot easier—everything you need is in the cookies.

Makes 15 to 18 three-inch cookies

1 cup (2 bars) crushed Butterfinger candy

1 cup crushed potato chips

4 cups all-purpose flour

1 teaspoon baking soda

1 teaspoon table salt

11 tablespoons (or ⅔ cup) unsalted butter, cold and cubed

11 tablespoons (or ⅔ cup) vegetable shortening, room temperature

1 cup sugar

1 cup packed light brown sugar

2 extra-large eggs, cold

1½ teaspoons pure vanilla extract

⅓ cup (3 ounces) semisweet chocolate chips

⅓ cup (3 ounces) peanut butter chips

½ cup crushed pretzels

Preheat the oven to 350°F.

In a small bowl, combine ½ cup of the crushed Butterfingers and ½ cup of the crushed potato chips. Set aside. This will serve as your topping for the cookies.

In a medium bowl, stir together the flour, baking soda, and salt. Set aside.

In a large mixing bowl or the bowl of a stand mixer, combine the butter, shortening, sugar, brown sugar, eggs, and vanilla extract and beat on medium-low speed until mixed with just small chunks of butter remaining, approximately 30 seconds. Every time you mix ingredients, scrape down the sides of the bowl with a spatula to be sure all ingredients are included in the mix—every bit matters! Add half of the dry ingredient mixture and mix on low speed until just incorporated and no flour is visible, about 30 seconds. Add half of the remaining dry ingredients and mix on low speed until the flour is incorporated and all butter chunks are gone, approximately 20 seconds. Add the remaining dry ingredients and mix until the dough pulls away from the sides of the bowl and is not sticky to the touch, about 20 seconds. Be careful not to overmix—that's how you get flat cookies. Stir in the chocolate chips, peanut butter chips, remaining crushed butterfingers and potato chips, and the crushed pretzels.

Line two baking sheets with parchment paper. Scoop the dough ⅓ cup at a time and firmly roll into round balls approximately 1½ inches in diameter. Place 6 cookies on each prepared baking sheet, spacing them out well. Bake on the middle and lower racks of the oven until the tops are a light golden brown and you notice hairline cracks forming on the sides, 12 to 14 minutes, spinning each pan 180 degrees and swapping their positions halfway through.

Let the cookies cool on the baking sheets for 10 minutes, then use a wide spatula to transfer them to a wire rack or parchment paper on the counter to cool completely. Let the baking sheets cool before repeating with the remaining cookies.

Store in an airtight container at room temperature for up to 4 days or freeze for up to a month.

APPLE OATMEAL COOKIES

When I was working with Williams Sonoma to develop baking mixes, we decided to do an original flavor exclusively for our partnership. We landed on apple oatmeal, which ended up being one of our customers' favorite mixes. I reverse engineered this one and developed my own recipe so we can all continue gracing our ovens with this delicious cookie. Honeycrisp apples are my favorite for this because they are the perfect mix of sweet and tart.

Makes 18 to 20 three-inch cookies

2 cups all-purpose flour

1 teaspoon baking powder

¼ teaspoon baking soda

½ teaspoon table salt

½ heaping teaspoon ground cinnamon

4 tablespoons (or ¼ cup) unsalted butter, cold and cubed

8 tablespoons (or ½ cup) vegetable shortening, room temperature

½ cup sugar

1 cup packed light brown sugar

2 extra-large eggs, cold

1½ teaspoons pure vanilla extract

1½ teaspoons apple juice

3½ cups rolled oats (not instant oats)

1½ cups finely diced apples (from about 2 medium apples)

Preheat the oven to 350°F.

In a medium bowl, stir together the flour, baking powder, baking soda, salt, and cinnamon. Set aside.

In a large mixing bowl or the bowl of a stand mixer, combine the butter, shortening, sugar, and brown sugar and beat on medium speed until creamed, approximately 1 minute. Scrape down the sides of the bowl with a spatula to be sure all ingredients are included in the mix—every bit matters! Add the eggs, vanilla extract, and apple juice and mix until combined and the mixture is smooth. Add the entire bowl of dry ingredients at once and mix on medium speed until it's fully combined and no flour is visible, about 1 minute. Scrape the sides of the bowl again. Add the oats and mix on low speed or stir by hand until just combined. Maintaining the integrity of the oats will help you get the perfect texture in your cookies. Stir in the apples.

Line two baking sheets with parchment paper. Scoop the dough ¼ cup at a time and place 8 cookies on each prepared baking sheet, spacing them out well. Using your fingers, gently flatten each cookie until they look like flat haystacks. The cookies won't spread when you bake them, so you want to shape them into their final desired form at this point. Bake on the middle and lower racks of the oven until the edges are just golden brown and the centers of the cookies no longer look wet, 11 to 13 minutes, spinning each pan 180 degrees and swapping their positions halfway through.

Let the cookies cool on the baking sheet for 10 minutes, then use a wide spatula to transfer them to a wire rack to cool completely. Let the baking sheets cool before repeating with the remaining cookies.

Store in an airtight container at room temperature for up to 4 days or freeze for up to a month.

ENGLISH TOFFEE COOKIES

The difference between American toffee and English toffee is the sugar. I personally prefer the flavor profile of English toffee, as it calls for more brown sugar, whereas American toffee usually calls for white sugar. This candy is an elegant addition to the blonde dough you've already learned to make. The toffee melts just enough in the oven, but still retains its trademark crunch. For the full experience, serve with a spot of tea. Cheerio!

Makes 15 to 18 three-inch cookies

2 cups (8 bars) finely chopped English toffee candy

4 cups all-purpose flour

1 teaspoon baking soda

1 teaspoon table salt

11 tablespoons (or ⅔ cup) unsalted butter, cold and cubed

11 tablespoons (or ⅔ cup) vegetable shortening, room temperature

1 cup sugar

1 cup packed light brown sugar

2 extra-large eggs, cold

1½ teaspoons pure vanilla extract

Preheat the oven to 350°F.

Set aside ½ cup of the finely chopped toffee candy in a small bowl. This will serve as your topping for the cookies.

In a medium bowl, stir together the flour, baking soda, and salt. Set aside.

In a large mixing bowl or the bowl of a stand mixer, combine the butter, shortening, sugar, brown sugar, eggs, and vanilla extract and beat on medium-low speed until mixed with just small chunks of butter remaining, approximately 30 seconds. Every time you mix ingredients, scrape down the sides of the bowl with a spatula to be sure all ingredients are included in the mix—every bit matters! Add half of the dry ingredient mixture and mix on low speed until just incorporated and no flour is visible, about 30 seconds. Add half of the remaining dry ingredients and mix on low speed until the flour is incorporated and all butter chunks are gone, approximately 20 seconds. Add the

remaining dry ingredients and mix until the dough pulls away from the sides of the bowl and is not sticky to the touch, about 20 seconds. Be careful not to overmix—that's how you get flat cookies. Stir in the toffee candy pieces.

Line two baking sheets with parchment paper. Scoop the dough ⅓ cup at a time and firmly roll into round balls approximately 1½ inches in diameter. Before placing 6 cookies on each prepared baking sheet, roll the top of each dough ball in the toffee bits you set aside. Bake on the middle and lower racks of the oven until the tops are a light golden brown and you notice hairline cracks forming on the sides, 12 to 14 minutes, spinning each pan 180 degrees and swapping their positions halfway through.

Let the cookies cool on the baking sheets for 10 minutes, then use a wide spatula to transfer them to a wire rack or parchment paper on the counter to cool completely. Let the baking sheets cool before repeating with the remaining cookies.

Store in an airtight container at room temperature for up to 4 days or freeze for up to a month.

MILK AND CEREAL COOKIES

❦

Whether it's the sugary kind or the healthy kind, cereal is one of my favorite snacks and meals. That love, coupled with nostalgia for the beloved childhood ritual of watching Saturday morning cartoons while eating sugary cereal, inspired the creation of this cookie. The yogurt chips give it a nice tangy creaminess, and the cereals unite to create that quintessential taste that will transport you back to simpler times. Feel free to have fun and experiment with your favorite cereals, but the teamwork between these five is stellar. Pairs best with a cold glass of milk and an episode of *Tom and Jerry*.

Makes 15 to 18 3-inch cookies

¾ cup **Golden Grahams cereal**, divided

¾ cup **Fruity Pebbles cereal**, divided

4 cups **all-purpose flour**

1 teaspoon **baking soda**

1 teaspoon **table salt**

11 tablespoons (or ⅔ cup) **unsalted butter**, cold and cubed

11 tablespoons (or ⅔ cup) **vegetable shortening**, room temperature

1 cup **sugar**

1 cup packed **light brown sugar**

2 extra-large **eggs**, cold

1½ teaspoons **pure vanilla extract**

1 cup (8 ounces) **yogurt chips**

¼ cup **Rice Krispies cereal**

¼ cup **Lucky Charms cereal**

¼ cup **Cap'n Crunch cereal**

Preheat the oven to 350°F.

In a small bowl and using your hands, crush ½ cup of the Golden Grahams into bits. Add ½ cup of the Fruity Pebbles to the bowl, stir, and set aside. This will serve as your topping for the cookies.

In a medium bowl, stir together the flour, baking soda, and salt. Set aside.

In a large mixing bowl or the bowl of a stand mixer, combine the butter, shortening, sugar, brown sugar, eggs, and vanilla extract and beat on medium-low speed until mixed with just small chunks of butter remaining, approximately 30 seconds. Every time you mix ingredients, scrape down the sides of the bowl with a spatula to be sure all ingredients are included in the mix—every bit matters! Add half of the dry ingredient mixture and mix on low speed until just incorporated and no flour is visible, about 30 seconds. Add half of the remaining dry ingredients and mix on low speed until the flour is incorporated and all butter chunks are gone, approximately 20 seconds. Add the remaining dry ingredients and mix until the dough pulls away from the sides of the bowl and is not sticky to the touch, about 20 seconds. Be careful not to overmix—that's how you get flat cookies. Mix in the yogurt chips and all the cereals.

Line two baking sheets with parchment paper. Scoop the dough ⅓ cup at a time and firmly roll into round balls approximately 1½ inches in diameter. Before placing 6 cookies on each prepared baking sheet, roll the top of each dough ball in your Fruity Pebble/Golden Grahams mixture. Bake on the middle and lower racks of the oven until the tops are a light golden brown and you notice hairline cracks forming on the sides, 12 to 14 minutes, spinning each pan 180 degrees and swapping their positions halfway through.

Let the cookies cool on the baking sheets for 10 minutes, then use a wide spatula to transfer them to a wire rack or parchment paper on the counter to cool completely. Let the baking sheets cool before repeating with the remaining cookies.

Store in an airtight container at room temperature for up to 4 days or freeze for up to a month.

LEMON BLUEBERRY COOKIES

The sweet, tangy flavor of blueberries and the zesty citrus of lemons are a magical combination. This fresh, summery creation has a balanced flavor that allows both fruits to shine while also complementing the other. The soft, lemony taste resembles an animal cracker and the blueberries add a little complexity. Freezing the blueberries will make them easier to place inside and on top of each cookie. Additionally, I highly recommend using tiny blueberries for the inside, as that allows the flavor to pervade the whole treat.

Makes 15 to 18 three-inch cookies

4 cups all-purpose flour	1 cup packed light brown sugar
1 teaspoon baking soda	2 extra-large eggs, cold
1 teaspoon table salt	1½ teaspoons pure vanilla extract
11 tablespoons (or ⅔ cup) unsalted butter, cold and cubed	1½ teaspoons pure lemon extract
11 tablespoons (or ⅔ cup) shortening, room temperature	2 cups fresh blueberries, frozen
1 cup sugar	

Preheat the oven to 350°F.

In a medium bowl, stir together the flour, baking soda, and salt. Set aside.

In a large mixing bowl or the bowl of a stand mixer, combine the butter, shortening, sugar, brown sugar, eggs, vanilla extract, and lemon extract and beat on medium-low speed until mixed with just small chunks of butter remaining, approximately 30 seconds. Every time you mix ingredients, scrape down the sides of the bowl with a spatula to be sure all ingredients are included in the mix—every bit matters! Add half of the dry ingredient mixture and mix on low speed until just incorporated and no flour is visible, about 30 seconds. Add half of the remaining dry ingredients and mix on low speed until the flour is incorporated and all butter chunks are gone, approximately 20 seconds. Add the remaining dry ingredients and mix until the dough pulls away from the sides of the bowl and is not sticky to the touch, about 20 seconds. Be careful not to overmix—that's how you get flat cookies.

Line two baking sheets with parchment paper. Scoop the dough ⅓ cup at a time and place 3 frozen blueberries in the middle of each scoop, making sure the berries are fully encased in dough. Firmly roll into round balls approximately 1½ inches in diameter. With the dough ball still in your hands, top each cookie with 3 more blueberries, gently pushing them in to keep them in position while they bake. Place 6 cookies on each prepared baking sheet, spacing them out well. Bake on the middle and lower racks of the oven until the tops are a light golden brown and you notice hairline cracks forming on the sides, 12 to 14 minutes, spinning each pan 180 degrees and swapping their positions halfway through.

Let the cookies cool on the baking sheets for 10 minutes, then use a wide spatula to transfer them to a wire rack or parchment paper on the counter to cool completely. Let the baking sheets cool before repeating with the remaining cookies.

Store in an airtight container at room temperature for up to 3 days or freeze for up to a month.

* NOTE: If you're living a life free from gluten, this is a delicious recipe to make gluten free! Substitute the flour for 4 cups plus 2 tablespoons of gluten-free baking flour (I prefer Cup4Cup). Given the way the blueberries react with the gluten-free flour, we do a GF Lemon Sugar Cookie at Milk Jar instead. Reduce your scoops to ¼ cup in size and roll the tops in coarse sugar before baking, and voila! You're in for a treat. One trick to get the gluten-free variation to bake perfectly is to mix the dough about 20 seconds longer when you add in the last of the flour mixture.

PEACH COBBLER COOKIES
—*with*—
STREUSEL TOPPING

As you've likely noticed, my inspiration for new cookie flavors comes from everywhere. This particular delight was inspired by the book *James and the Giant Peach*, in honor of author Roald Dahl's one-hundredth birthday. (May he rest in peace!) The peaches are accented by the creamy yogurt chips and join forces with the streusel to create cobbler in cookie form. It's truly on its own level. I strongly recommend that you double or triple the streusel recipe and keep it on hand to use as an ice cream topping or even just to eat with a spoon. It's that good!

Makes 15 to 18 three-inch cookies

FOR THE STREUSEL TOPPING:

¾ cup all-purpose flour

½ cup packed light brown sugar

½ teaspoon ground cinnamon

⅓ cup unsalted butter, cold and cubed

FOR THE COOKIES:

1–2 fresh peaches, sliced

4 cups all-purpose flour

1 teaspoon baking soda

1 teaspoon table salt

11 tablespoons (or ⅔ cup) unsalted butter, cold and cubed

11 tablespoons (or ⅔ cup) vegetable shortening, room temperature

1 cup sugar

1 cup packed light brown sugar

2 extra-large eggs, cold

1½ teaspoons pure vanilla extract

1½ teaspoons pure peach extract

1¾ cups (14 ounces) yogurt chips

TO MAKE THE TOPPING: In a medium bowl, whisk together the flour, brown sugar, and cinnamon. Add the butter, and using your fingers, pinch it all together until it forms a crumble. This can be made up to 3 days ahead of time; just store in an airtight container, refrigerate, and stir before using.

TO MAKE THE COOKIES: Preheat the oven to 350°F.

Wash the peaches and dry them thoroughly with paper towel. Slice the peaches into quarter-sized pieces and place them on a plate or tray lined with paper towel. Set aside.

In a medium bowl, stir together the flour, baking soda, and salt. Set aside.

In a large mixing bowl or the bowl of a stand mixer, combine the butter, shortening, sugar, brown sugar, eggs, vanilla extract, and peach extract and beat on medium-low speed until mixed with just small chunks of butter remaining, approximately 30 seconds. Every time you mix ingredients, scrape down the sides of the bowl with a spatula to be sure all ingredients are included in the mix—every bit matters! Add half of the dry ingredient mixture and mix on low speed until just incorporated and no flour is visible, about 30 seconds. Add half of the remaining dry ingredients and mix on low speed until the flour is incorporated and all butter chunks are gone, approximately 20 seconds. Add the remaining dry ingredients and mix until the dough pulls away from the sides of the bowl and is not sticky to the touch, about 20 seconds. Be careful not to overmix—that's how you get flat cookies. Stir in the yogurt chips.

Line two baking sheets with parchment paper. Scoop the dough ⅓ cup at a time and place 2 peach slices in the middle of each scoop, making sure the fruit is fully encased in dough. Firmly roll into round balls approximately 1½ inches in diameter. Before placing 6 cookies on each prepared baking sheet, roll the top of each dough ball in the streusel mixture and, with the dough ball still in your hands, top each cookie with a second peach slice, gently pushing it in to keep it in position while the cookies bake. Bake on the middle and lower racks of the oven until you notice hairline cracks forming on the sides, approximately 12 to 14 minutes, spinning each pan 180 degrees and swapping their positions halfway through.

Let the cookies cool on the baking sheets for 10 minutes, then use a wide spatula to transfer them to a wire rack or parchment paper on the counter to cool completely. Let the baking sheets cool before repeating with the remaining cookies.

Store in an airtight container at room temperature for up to 2 days or freeze for up to a month.

CHOCOLATE-COVERED STRAWBERRY COOKIES

This fresh take on the classic Valentine's Day treat is one of my most beautiful cookies. From cutting the strawberries into hearts to melting the chocolate and drizzling it over each cookie, this recipe involves several steps that take a few extra minutes, but what better way to show love for yourself or someone else than to dedicate a little extra time? Allowing the chocolate drizzle to cool completely and harden over the roasted strawberry is a big part of the experience with this cookie. There's something decadent about biting into the thick chocolate coating of a chocolate-covered strawberry, and this cookie replicates that sensation deliciously.

Makes 15 to 18 three-inch cookies

15 fresh strawberries, quartered and halved

3½ cups all-purpose flour

⅓ cup natural unsweetened cocoa powder

1 teaspoon baking soda

1 teaspoon table salt

11 tablespoons (or ⅔ cup) unsalted butter, cold and cubed

11 tablespoons (or ⅔ cup) vegetable shortening, room temperature

1 cup sugar

1 cup packed light brown sugar

2 extra-large eggs, cold

1½ teaspoons pure vanilla extract

2¾ cups (22 ounces) semisweet chocolate chips, divided

Preheat the oven to 350°F.

Wash the strawberries and dry thoroughly with paper towel. Quarter 5 strawberries and place them on a plate or tray lined with paper towel. Halve the remaining 10 strawberries. Using a paring knife, carve each half into a heart. Place on the paper towel–lined plate and set aside.

In a medium bowl, stir together the flour, cocoa powder, baking soda, and salt. Set aside.

In a large mixing bowl or the bowl of a stand mixer, combine the butter, shortening, sugar, brown sugar, eggs, and vanilla extract and beat on medium-low speed until mixed with just small chunks of butter remaining, approximately 30 seconds. Every time you mix ingredients, scrape down the sides of the bowl with a spatula to be sure all ingredients are included in the mix—every bit matters! Add half of the dry ingredient mixture and mix on low speed until just incorporated and no flour is visible, about 30 seconds. Add half of the remaining dry ingredients and mix on low speed until the flour is incorporated and all butter chunks are gone, approximately 20 seconds. Add the remaining dry ingredients and mix until the dough pulls away from the sides of the bowl and is not sticky to the touch, about 20 seconds. Be careful not to overmix—that's how you get flat cookies. Stir in 1¾ cups of the chocolate chips.

Line two baking sheets with parchment paper. Scoop the dough ⅓ cup at a time and place a strawberry quarter in the middle of each scoop, making sure the berry is fully encased in dough. Firmly roll into round balls approximately 1½ inches in diameter. With the dough ball still in your hands, top each cookie with a strawberry heart, gently pushing it in to keep it in position while the cookies bake. Place 6 cookies on each prepared baking sheet, spacing them out well. Bake on the middle and lower oven racks until you notice hairline cracks forming on the sides, 11 to 13 minutes, spinning each pan 180 degrees and swapping their positions halfway through.

Let the cookies cool on the baking sheets for 10 minutes, then use a wide spatula to transfer them to a wire rack or parchment paper on the counter to cool completely. Let the baking sheets cool before repeating with the remaining cookies.

When the cookies have cooled completely, it's time to drizzle and top them! In a small, microwave-safe bowl, melt the remaining 1 cup chocolate chips in 30-second increments, stirring each time. Once the chocolate is melted, transfer to a piping bag with a skinny tip attached. Alternately, transfer to a plastic storage bag, work all the chocolate into one corner, and snip the corner off. In a zig-zag motion and working from one side of each cookie to the other, drizzle the tops with chocolate. To accelerate the hardening of the chocolate and really achieve that "chocolate-covered" sensation, place your cookies in the refrigerator for 5 minutes before serving.

Store in an airtight container at room temperature for up to 2 days or freeze for up to a month.

Scan for Video!

PEPPERMINT BARK COOKIES

When developing Milk Jar's seasonal flavor for December, I knew it had to be my favorite holiday confection in cookie form. The way the cool peppermint dough hugs the gooey chocolate while the candy cane bits melt into a chewy surprise is like waking up on Christmas morning to a blanket of snow outside. Magical. If you can't purchase crushed candy cane, you can crush mini candy canes using a food processor.

Makes 18 to 20 three-inch cookies

4 cups all-purpose flour

1 teaspoon baking soda

1 teaspoon table salt

11 tablespoons (or ⅔ cup) unsalted butter, cold and cubed

11 tablespoons (or ⅔ cup) vegetable shortening, room temperature

1 cup sugar

1 cup packed light brown sugar

2 extra-large eggs, cold

1½ teaspoons pure vanilla extract

1½ teaspoons pure peppermint extract

¾ cup (6 ounces) semisweet chocolate chips

¾ cup (6 ounces) white chocolate chips

¾ cup (6 ounces) crushed candy cane

Preheat the oven to 350°F.

In a medium bowl, stir together the flour, baking soda, and salt. Set aside.

In a large mixing bowl or the bowl of a stand mixer, combine the butter, shortening, sugar, brown sugar, eggs, vanilla extract, and peppermint extract and beat on medium-low speed until mixed with just small chunks of butter remaining, approximately 30 seconds. Every time you mix ingredients, scrape down the sides of the bowl with a spatula to be sure all ingredients are included in the mix—every bit matters! Add half of the dry ingredient mixture and mix on low speed until just incorporated and no flour is visible, about 30 seconds. Add half of the remaining dry ingredients and mix on low speed until the flour is incorporated and all butter chunks are gone, approximately 20 seconds. Add the remaining dry ingredients and mix until the dough pulls away from the sides of the bowl and is not sticky to the touch, about 20 seconds. Be careful not to overmix—that's how you get flat cookies. Stir in the chocolate chips, white chocolate chips, and candy cane.

Line two baking sheets with parchment paper. Scoop the dough ⅓ cup at a time and firmly roll into round balls approximately 1½ inches in diameter. Place 6 cookies on each prepared baking sheet, spacing them out well. Bake on the middle and lower racks of the oven until the tops are a light golden brown and you notice hairline cracks forming on the sides, 12 to 14 minutes, spinning each pan 180 degrees and swapping their positions halfway through.

Let the cookies cool on the baking sheets for 10 minutes, then use a wide spatula to transfer them to a wire rack or parchment paper on the counter to cool completely. Let the baking sheets cool before repeating with the remaining cookies.

Store in an airtight container at room temperature for up to 4 days or freeze for up to a month.

---

* NOTE: If you're living a life free from gluten, this is an easy recipe to make gluten free! Simply substitute the all-purpose flour with 4 cups plus 2 tablespoons of gluten-free baking flour (I prefer Cup4Cup brand) and reduce the chocolate chips to 1¾ cups. One trick to get the gluten-free version to bake perfectly is to mix the dough about 20 seconds longer when you add in the last of the flour mixture.

Scan for Tunes!

YOUR NEW FAVORITE CHOCOLATE CAKE
—*with*—
CHOCOLATE FUDGE FROSTING

As you might guess, I like my desserts decadent. I mean, if you're going to eat sweets, make it count, right?! There is something irresistible about a dense chocolate cake, and I loved the experimentation that led me to this recipe. Given that I've dedicated most of my life's baking time to cookies, playing with the chemistry of cakes is a welcome change. I tried various cocoa powders, different fats, and various temperatures of ingredients until I created the frosted chocolate cake of my dreams. The cake itself is superbly moist, heavy on the chocolate, and when coupled with the flawlessly fudgy frosting, leaves you craving a slice of this on the regular. If you are looking for a cake with a little more drama, make it three-tiered by dividing the batter into three cake pans instead of two.

Makes one 2- or 3-layer cake

Butter for greasing the pans

1½ cups sugar

½ cup packed light brown sugar

2 cups all-purpose flour, plus more for the pans if needed

½ cup natural unsweetened cocoa powder

½ cup Hershey's Special Dark Dutched cocoa powder

2 teaspoons baking soda

1 teaspoon baking powder

1 teaspoon table salt

¾ cup vegetable oil

1 cup boiling water

1 cup whole milk, room temperature

1 tablespoon pure vanilla extract

2 large eggs, room temperature

Chocolate Fudge Frosting (recipe follows)

Preheat the oven to 350°F and butter and line two 9-inch-round cake pans with parchment paper. Alternatively, butter and flour the pans, making sure you shake out all the excess flour.

In a large mixing bowl, combine the sugar, brown sugar, flour, cocoas, baking soda, baking powder, and salt and whisk until thoroughly combined.

Add the oil, boiling water, milk, and vanilla extract and beat with an electric mixer on medium speed until all dry ingredients are incorporated into the batter. Now, mix in the eggs so they don't get cooked by the boiling water.

Divide the batter evenly between the two prepared pans. Bake for 30 to 35 minutes, until a toothpick inserted into the center of the cakes comes out clean. Allow the cakes to cool for about 10 minutes in the pans and then remove them from the pans to cool completely on a wire rack.

Frost and decorate as desired using the delicious Chocolate Fudge Frosting.

Store covered in the refrigerator for up to 4 days.

If you want to bake the cakes ahead of time and frost later, wrap each cooled cake securely with plastic wrap and freeze for up to a month. When you're ready to ice it, remove them from the freezer and allow to defrost on the counter.

CHOCOLATE FUDGE FROSTING

Makes 4 cups

6½ cups powdered sugar

¾ cup Hershey's Special Dark Dutched cocoa powder

¾ cup whole milk, plus more as desired

2 teaspoons pure vanilla extract

1 cup (2 sticks) unsalted butter, room temperature

1½ cups (12 ounces) semisweet chocolate chips

In the bowl of a stand mixer fitted with the paddle attachment, combine the powdered sugar and cocoa. Let the mixer run for a few seconds to fully blend them. Set aside.

In a heat-resistant glass measuring cup, mix together the milk and vanilla extract. Set aside.

In a covered small saucepan on low heat, melt the butter and chocolate chips, stirring frequently. As the chocolate really starts to melt, stir constantly. It will take about 10 minutes for the chocolate chips to completely melt, but it's important to take it slow and keep the temperature on low. When it's melted and smooth, whisk in the milk and vanilla extract until fully incorporated. Transfer the melted chocolate mixture to the glass measuring cup.

With the mixer running on medium speed, slowly pour the melted chocolate mixture into the powdered sugar mixture until all of it is completely incorporated and the frosting reaches its delicious, fudgy consistency and takes on a beautiful sheen. If you like your frosting a little thinner, you can mix in more milk, 1 tablespoon at a time.

Use immediately or store in an airtight container in the refrigerator for up to 3 days. To get the frosting back to a spreadable consistency, allow it to return to room temperature and then microwave in 30-second increments, stirring each time. Allow to cool before spreading.

CHOCOLATE CHIP COOKIE CAKE

The only thing better than a cookie is a giant cookie . . . covered in frosting. The perfect celebration cake for the cookie lover in your life or just dessert on a Tuesday, this is my Milk Jar spin on the quintessential mall offering that I coveted as a kid. To get that signature Milk Jar doughy goodness, be sure you don't overbake your cakes. The edges will be golden brown, but the center will still look shiny. Here's to bringing out your inner child.

Note: This recipe makes enough dough for a two-layer cookie cake (or two individual cakes), but feel free to make one cake and freeze the other half of the dough or make cookies with it.

Makes two 9-inch cakes

11 tablespoons (or ⅔ cup) unsalted butter, cold and cubed, plus more for greasing the pan

4 cups all-purpose flour, plus more for the pan if needed

11 tablespoons (or ⅔ cup) vegetable shortening, room temperature

1 cup sugar

1 cup packed light brown sugar

½ teaspoon baking soda

1 teaspoon table salt

2 extra-large eggs, cold

1½ teaspoons pure vanilla extract

2 cups (16 ounces) semisweet chocolate chips

White Frosting or Chocolate Fudge Frosting (recipes on pages 102 or 92)

Preheat the oven to 350°F and butter and line two 9-inch springform pans with parchment paper. Alternatively, butter and flour the pan, making sure you shake out all the excess flour.

In a medium bowl, measure out the flour. Set aside.

In a large mixing bowl with a wooden spoon or a stand mixer with the paddle attachment, combine the butter, shortening, sugar, brown sugar, baking soda, salt, eggs, and vanilla extract and beat on medium-low speed until mixed but with small chunks of

butter remaining, approximately 1 minute. After each mix, scrape down the sides of the bowl with a spatula to be sure all ingredients are included in the mix—every bit matters! Add half of the flour and mix until just incorporated and no flour is visible. Add half of the remaining flour and mix until the flour is incorporated and all butter chunks are gone. Add the remaining flour and mix until the dough pulls away from the sides of the bowl and is not sticky to the touch. Stir in chocolate chips with a spatula.

Divide the dough in half and transfer to the pans. Using your fingers, firmly flatten the dough, pressing down evenly. Bake on the middle rack of the oven for 28 to 30 minutes, until golden brown. Allow to cool completely in the pans. Run a knife around the edge before removing the side of each springform pan.

Frost and decorate as you wish using the White Frosting or the Chocolate Fudge Frosting. Slice and serve with a scoop of ice cream!

Store covered at room temperature for up to 4 days or freeze for up to a month.

---

* NOTE: If you're living a life free from gluten, this is an easy recipe to make gluten free! Simply substitute the all-purpose flour for 4 cups plus 2 tablespoons of gluten-free baking flour (I prefer Cup4Cup brand) and reduce the chocolate chips to 1¾ cups. One trick to get the gluten-free version to bake perfectly is to mix the dough about 20 seconds longer when you add in the last of the flour mixture.

BETTER THAN ALMOST ANYTHING CAKE

My mom would make this cake for potlucks, pitch-ins, and school events. Commonly referred to as Better Than Sex Cake, my mom coined the G-rated version Better Than Almost Anything Cake. Adorable. And while this version of the recipe shows you how to make the whole cake from scratch, you can always use mom's shortcut and buy boxed German chocolate cake mix and Cool Whip. Either way, save me a slice!

Makes one 13 by 9-inch cake

Butter for greasing the pan

2 cups sugar

1¾ cups all-purpose flour, plus more for the pan if needed

¾ cup natural unsweetened cocoa powder

1½ teaspoons baking soda

1½ teaspoons baking powder

1 teaspoon table salt

½ cup vegetable oil

1 cup buttermilk

2 large eggs

1 tablespoon pure vanilla extract

1 cup boiling water

1 (14-ounce) can sweetened condensed milk

1 (16-ounce) jar caramel or fudge topping (Ghirardelli is my go-to)

2 cups Crème de la Cloud (recipe on page 135)

1 (8-ounce) bag toffee chips

Preheat the oven to 350°F and butter and line a 13 by 9-inch cake pan with parchment paper. Alternatively, butter and flour the pan, making sure you shake out all the excess flour.

In a large mixing bowl, combine the sugar, flour, cocoa, baking soda, baking powder, and salt, whisking until thoroughly combined.

In a medium mixing bowl, combine the oil, buttermilk, eggs, and vanilla and beat with an electric mixer on medium speed until all the ingredients are incorporated. Add this mixture to the dry ingredients and mix thoroughly. Stir in the boiling water.

Pour the batter into the cake pan. Bake for 35 to 38 minutes, until a toothpick inserted into the center of the cake comes out clean. Allow to cool for 15 minutes.

Utilizing the handle of a wooden spoon or spatula, poke holes an inch apart to form a grid across the top of the cake. Pour the condensed milk all over the top of the cake and let stand until it is absorbed. Drizzle caramel or fudge evenly over the top of the cake. At this point, run a knife along the edges of the pan to loosen the cake. Cover and refrigerate for 2½ hours.

While the cake is chilling, make your Crème de la Cloud topping and refrigerate it, too.

Spread the topping over the entire cake, sprinkle with toffee chips, and serve! (I'll let you be the judge if it's better than "almost anything.")

Store covered in the refrigerator for up to 4 days.

CONFETTI CAKE

~with~

WHITE FROSTING

Make any day a fête by baking this beauty. It's light, fluffy, and joyous—just like confetti! If you've never heard of "quin" sprinkles, they are the disc-shaped sprinkles that look like mini Necco wafers and, well, confetti. Party on and cue the gasps of delight when you slice into this cake!

Makes one 3-layer cake

3½ cups all-purpose flour

2 teaspoons baking powder

½ teaspoon table salt

1 cup (2 sticks) unsalted butter, softened

½ cup vegetable shortening, room temperature

3 cups sugar

1 cup whole milk, room temperature

1 tablespoon pure vanilla extract

9 egg whites

½ cup quin sprinkles (edible confetti)

White Frosting (recipe follows)

Preheat the oven to 350°F and butter and line three 9-inch round cake pans with parchment paper. Alternatively, butter and flour the pans, making sure you shake out all the excess flour.

In a large mixing bowl, sift together the flour, baking powder, and salt and set aside.

In a large mixing bowl with a wooden spoon or the bowl of a stand mixer with the paddle attachment, cream the butter and shortening until fluffy, 3 to 4 minutes. Add the sugar 1 cup at a time and mix, making sure each cup is fully incorporated before adding the next.

In a small bowl or measuring cup, whisk the milk and vanilla extract together with a fork.

Starting and ending with the flour mixture, alternately add the flour and milk mixtures to the butter mixture in the large bowl of stand mixer, gently stirring after each addition to combine.

In a separate bowl and using either a hand mixer or stand mixer with the whisk attachment, beat the egg whites on high speed until stiff peaks form. Gently fold into the batter. Sprinkle the quin sprinkles into the batter and stir once or twice to incorporate them. Stirring too much will cause the colors to bleed and turn your pretty white batter a grayish hue.

Divide the batter evenly among the three prepared cake pans. Bake for 25 to 28 minutes, until a toothpick inserted into the center of the cakes comes out clean. Remove and allow to cool for about 10 minutes in the pans and then cool completely on a wire rack.

Frost and decorate as desired using the delicious White Frosting recipe. Store covered in the refrigerator for up to 4 days.

If you want to bake the cakes ahead of time and frost later, wrap each cooled cake securely with plastic wrap and freeze for up to a month. When you're ready to ice it, remove them from the freezer and allow to defrost on the counter.

WHITE FROSTING

Makes 2½ cups

¾ cup (1½ sticks) unsalted butter, softened	1 tablespoon whole milk
1 teaspoon pure vanilla extract	1 pound (3⅔ cups) powdered sugar

Using a hand mixer or a stand mixer with the paddle attachment, cream the butter. Add the vanilla extract and milk and mix. Slowly beat in the powdered sugar until all of it is completely incorporated and the frosting is smooth.

Use immediately or store in an airtight container in the refrigerator for up to 3 days. To get the frosting back to a spreadable consistency, allow it to return to room temperature and stir well.

CARROT CAKE

—with—

CREAM CHEESE FROSTING

❦

My biggest gripes about carrot cakes have always been the overpowering flavor of the cream cheese frosting and how a lot of them have too much going on in the cake part—raisins, pineapple, etc. This light, fluffy, and incredibly flavorful cake and its accompanying frosting provide you a deliciously balanced dessert, plus it's a great way to get your kids to eat their vegetables. *wink*

❧ *Makes one 2-layer cake* ❧

Butter for greasing the pans

2¼ cups all-purpose flour, plus more for the pans if needed

2 teaspoons baking powder

1 teaspoon baking soda

1 teaspoon table salt

1 tablespoon ground cinnamon

½ teaspoon ground nutmeg

¼ teaspoon ground cloves

1 cup sugar

1 cup packed light brown sugar

1¼ cups vegetable oil

4 extra-large eggs

1 tablespoon pure vanilla extract

2½ cups grated carrots (about 4½ ounces)

1 cup unsweetened grated coconut

¾ cup walnuts, chopped

Cream Cheese Frosting (recipe follows)

Preheat the oven to 350°F and butter and line two 9-inch-round cake pans with parchment paper.

Alternatively, butter and flour the pans, making sure you shake out all the excess flour.

In a medium mixing bowl, combine the flour, baking powder, baking soda, salt, cinnamon, nutmeg, and cloves. Set aside.

In a large mixing bowl with a wooden spoon or bowl of a stand mixer with the paddle attachment, combine the sugar, brown sugar, oil, eggs, and vanilla extract and mix until fully combined and smooth. Add the flour mixture all at once and mix until just combined. Fold in the carrots, coconut, and walnuts and stir until evenly distributed.

Divide the batter evenly between the two cake pans. Bake for 25 to 28 minutes, until a toothpick inserted into the center of the cakes comes out clean. Remove and allow to cool for about 10 minutes in the pans and then cool completely on a wire rack.

Frost and decorate as desired using the perfectly creamy Cream Cheese Frosting.

Store covered in the refrigerator for up to 4 days.

If you want to bake the cakes ahead of time and frost later, wrap each cooled cake securely with plastic wrap and freeze for up to a month. When you're ready to ice it, remove them from the freezer and allow to defrost on the counter.

CREAM CHEESE FROSTING

Makes 4 cups

½ cup (1 stick) unsalted butter, room temperature

8 ounces cream cheese, room temperature

2 teaspoons pure vanilla extract

1 tablespoon heavy cream

5 cups powdered sugar

Using an electric hand mixer or a stand mixer with the paddle attachment, cream the butter and cream cheese. Add the vanilla extract and cream and mix to incorporate. Mix in the powdered sugar, 1 cup at a time, until all of the sugar is completely incorporated and the frosting is smooth and creamy.

Use immediately or store in an airtight container in the refrigerator for up to 2 days. Allow to return to room temperature and stir well before using.

PERFECTLY FUDGY BROWNIES

ich, fudgy chocolate inside with that perfectly crisp top layer, these brownies are a quick go-to for a weeknight dessert or casual weekend gathering. If you're looking for more of a chewy brownie, simply bake for five additional minutes, then refrigerate.

Makes 9 to 12 brownies, depending on how big you cut them

2 bars (8 ounces) semisweet baking chocolate

¾ cup (1½ sticks) unsalted butter, melted

½ cup sugar

½ cup packed light brown sugar

2 extra-large eggs, cold

1 tablespoon pure vanilla extract

1 cup all-purpose flour

⅓ cup natural unsweetened cocoa powder

1 teaspoon table salt

Preheat the oven to 350°F and line an 8-inch square baking pan with parchment paper.

Using a knife, chop one chocolate bar into small chunks and set aside. Chop the second chocolate bar into small chunks and melt in a small saucepan on the stovetop or in the microwave in 20-second intervals. Set aside.

In a large bowl, mix the butter, sugar, and brown sugar with an electric hand mixer, then add the eggs and vanilla extract and mix for 1 to 2 minutes, until the mixture becomes fluffy.

Whisk in the melted chocolate, then sift in the flour, cocoa powder, and salt. Fold in the dry ingredients with a spatula. Be careful not to overmix or the brownies will develop more of a cake-like texture.

Fold in the remaining chopped chocolate chunks, then transfer the batter to the prepared baking pan.

Bake for 20 to 25 minutes, depending on how fudgy you like your brownies. Allow to cool, cut into squares, and enjoy! Store covered at room temperature for up to 4 days or freeze for up to a month.

Scan for Video!

CHEESECAKE
~with~
CHERRY COMPOTE TOPPING

The first cheesecake I made was for a colleague's birthday many years ago. I was very intimidated by the baking process (what on earth was a water bath?!), but I loved the new challenge. I have played around with this recipe a bit and think this is the creamiest, most delicious cheesecake. It's quite the process, but it is SO worth it. Take your time, follow the instructions, and you'll feel like a total champ as you eat the fruits of your labor. If cherries are out of season when you make this, you can substitute two 10-ounce bags of frozen cherries for the fresh.

Makes one 9-inch cake

FOR THE COMPOTE:

4½ cups cherries, pitted

½ cup sugar

2 tablespoons fresh lemon juice

5 tablespoons cornstarch

½ teaspoon salt

1 teaspoon pure vanilla extract

FOR THE CRUST:

2 cups (16 ounces) graham cracker crumbs

½ cup (1 stick) unsalted butter, melted, plus more for greasing the pan

¼ cup sugar

¼ teaspoon table salt

FOR THE FILLING:

4 (8-ounce) packages cream cheese, room temperature

¾ cup sugar

½ cup packed light brown sugar

1 teaspoon salt

1 tablespoon vanilla extract

4 large eggs, room temperature

½ cup sour cream, room temperature

½ cup heavy cream

TO MAKE THE CHERRY TOPPING: In a Dutch oven, combine the cherries, sugar, lemon juice, cornstarch, 4 tablespoons water, and the salt. Over medium-low heat, slowly bring the cherry mixture to a simmer, stirring regularly. Simmer for 3 to 5 minutes, until thick. Remove from the heat and stir in the vanilla extract. Let cool completely, then refrigerate until you're ready to top the cheesecake, up to 2 days.

TO MAKE THE CHEESECAKE: Preheat the oven to 350°F and grease a 9-inch springform pan.

In a medium bowl, mix together the graham cracker crumbs, butter, sugar, and salt. When well combined and starting to look like wet sand, transfer to the springform pan. Using your fingers, press the mixture firmly into the pan, fully covering the bottom and going up the sides of the pan a bit. Place the pan on a baking sheet and bake the crust for 10 minutes. Set aside to cool.

If making the crust ahead of time, wrap securely in plastic wrap and refrigerate up to 2 days or freeze for up to a month. Thaw before filling and baking.

Reduce the oven temperature to 325°F. Bring a large saucepan of water to a simmer. Cover and keep hot.

Triple wrap the springform pan with heavy-duty aluminum foil to protect the crust from the water bath you'll be baking it in. Once wrapped, place the springform pan in a roasting pan.

In a large mixing bowl with a wooden spoon or the bowl of a stand mixer with the paddle attachment, beat the cream cheese until smooth. Add the sugar and brown sugar and beat on medium speed until creamed. Add the salt, vanilla, and eggs and mix on low speed until fully combined. Add the sour cream and mix on low speed until incorporated. Last, add the heavy cream and mix on low speed until combined.

Pour the filling mixture into the crust. Place the roasting pan in the oven on the middle rack and pour in approximately ¾ inch of the hot water, surrounding the springform pan. (Make sure the water level is lower than the aluminum foil barrier.) Bake for 1½ hours to 1 hour 35 minutes, until the edges are set but the center still jiggles a little. Turn the oven off and open the door slightly. Allow the cheesecake to cool down in the oven for 1 hour.

Carefully remove the roasting pan from the oven and then remove the cheesecake from the roasting pan. Peel the aluminum foil away, cover the cake, and refrigerate for at least 4 hours. Before serving, run a knife around the edge of the cake and remove the springform sides. Top with the cherry topping, slice, and enjoy!

Store covered in the refrigerator for up to 4 days.

STRAWBERRY SHORTCAKE

My love of strawberry shortcake didn't stop with the cartoon character, for which I had quite the affinity— Mom made this dessert regularly and I was excited to develop my own take on it. I love these biscuits because they are just sweet enough and provide the perfect base for the strawberries and whipped cream. It's a super-simple treat to make and share with friends. And, as Strawberry Shortcake herself said, "Sharing is delicious."

Makes 8 to 10, depending how big you cut the biscuits

FOR THE STRAWBERRY FILLING:

6 cups fresh strawberries, quartered

¼ cup sugar

½ teaspoon fresh lemon juice

FOR THE BISCUITS:

3 cups all-purpose flour, plus more for dusting

¼ cup sugar

2 tablespoons baking powder

1 teaspoon table salt

¾ cup (1½ sticks) unsalted butter, cold and cubed

1 teaspoon pure vanilla extract

1 cup buttermilk plus 2 tablespoons for brushing the tops

Coarse sugar for sprinkling

FOR WHIPPED CREAM:

See recipe on page 132

TO MAKE THE STRAWBERRY FILLING: In a medium bowl, combine the strawberries, sugar, and lemon juice and stir until the sugar dissolves. Cover and place in the refrigerator until you're ready to serve, up to 2 days.

TO MAKE THE BISCUITS: Preheat the oven to 425°F. Line a baking sheet with parchment paper.

In a large mixing bowl, whisk together the flour, sugar, baking powder, and salt. Using a pastry cutter or a fork, cut in the butter.

In a small bowl or liquid measuring cup, stir the vanilla extract into 1 cup of the buttermilk. Pour into the flour mixture and stir until just combined.

Transfer the dough to a floured surface and, using your hands, flatten down until approximately 1 inch thick. Using a lightly floured biscuit cutter, cut out your biscuits by pushing straight down, then lifting straight up. Try not to twist the cutter, as this will affect how much your biscuits rise. Place them closely together on the prepared baking sheet. Brush the tops of each biscuit with the remaining 2 tablespoons buttermilk and sprinkle with coarse sugar. Bake for 13 to 15 minutes, until golden brown.

When the biscuits have cooled, cut each one in half and layer them with the strawberries and whipped cream to your liking.

Store the biscuits in an airtight container at room temperature for up to 3 days or freeze for up to a month.

HAZEL'S GERMAN CHOCOLATE CAKE
—with—
COCONUT PECAN FROSTING

Sometimes the only way to properly entertain is to finish the evening with a baked-from-scratch showstopper. This recipe was passed down by Adam's grandmother, and while I never had the pleasure of meeting her, I can tell she was a woman of taste. Her version of this classic is so, so good. The mild chocolate flavor and the sweet crunch of the shredded coconut frosting come together to make a cake that wows the crowd every time.

Makes one 3-layer cake

1 cup (2 sticks) unsalted butter, room temperature, plus more for the pans

4 ounces Baker's German's Sweet Chocolate, roughly chopped

2½ cups all-purpose flour, plus more for the pans if needed

1 teaspoon baking soda

¼ teaspoon table salt

2 cups sugar

4 egg whites, room temperature

4 egg yolks, beaten

1 teaspoon pure vanilla extract

1 cup buttermilk

Coconut Pecan Frosting (recipe follows)

Preheat the oven to 350°F and butter and line three 9-inch-round cake pans with parchment paper. Alternatively, butter and flour the pans, making sure you shake out all the excess flour.

In a small pot, bring ½ cup water to a boil. Add the chocolate and remove from the heat. Stir constantly until the chocolate is fully melted. Set aside to cool.

In a medium mixing bowl, sift together the flour, baking soda, and salt. Set aside.

In a small mixing bowl, beat the egg whites with an electric hand mixer until stiff peaks form, approximately 5 minutes. Set aside.

In a large mixing bowl, cream the butter and sugar with the electric mixer. Add the beaten egg yolks and mix until combined. Mix in the melted chocolate and vanilla extract.

Starting and ending with the flour mixture, alternately add the flour mixture and the buttermilk, mixing after each addition to combine. Gently fold in the beaten egg whites until combined.

Divide the batter evenly among the three cake pans. Bake for 25 to 30 minutes, until a toothpick inserted into the center of the cakes comes out clean. Let the cakes cool for about 10 minutes in the pans and then turn out and cool completely on wire racks.

Frost as desired using the Coconut Pecan Frosting.

Store covered in the refrigerator for up to 4 days.

If you want to bake the cakes ahead of time and frost later, wrap each cooled cake securely with plastic wrap and freeze for up to a month. When you're ready to ice it, remove them from the freezer and allow to defrost on the counter.

COCONUT PECAN FROSTING

Makes 3 cups

3 egg yolks

1 tablespoon all-purpose flour

1 cup sugar

¼ teaspoon salt

1 cup heavy cream

½ cup (1 stick) unsalted butter

1 cup unsweetened shredded coconut

1 cup pecan pieces

1 teaspoon pure vanilla extract

In a small mixing bowl, beat the egg yolks with a fork or whisk. Set aside.

In a small saucepan, combine the flour, sugar, salt, cream, and butter. Cook over low heat, stirring regularly, until the butter is melted and the mixture resembles syrup. Temper a small amount of the hot mixture into the beaten egg yolks, whisking constantly, then stir the egg yolk mixture into the saucepan. Add the coconut and pecan pieces. Continue cooking over low heat, stirring constantly, until the icing thickens to your desired consistency. Stir in vanilla extract. Let cool completely before frosting your cake.

Use immediately or store in an airtight container in the refrigerator for up to 2 days. Allow to return to room temperature before using.

THE PERFECT PIECRUST

A delicious pie starts with a great crust. I have tinkered with piecrusts over the years, and this one checks all the boxes for me: it's flaky and buttery, has a hint of sweetness, and beautifully complements pies of all kinds. Make sure you use very cold butter and don't skip the chilling steps.

Makes two 9-inch piecrusts

3 cups all-purpose flour, plus more for rolling	8 tablespoons (½ cup) vegetable shortening
1 teaspoon table salt	½ teaspoon pure vanilla extract
1½ teaspoons sugar	10–12 tablespoons ice water
12 tablespoons (1 cup) unsalted butter, cold	1 egg white, lightly beaten

In a large bowl, whisk together the flour, salt, and sugar.

Cube your butter and then, using a pastry cutter or two forks, immediately cut the butter into the dry ingredients, along with the shortening. You'll know you're done when you have a bowl of pea-sized clumps. Stir in the vanilla extract and 10 tablespoons of the ice water until just combined. If there is still flour that isn't incorporating, add up to 2 more tablespoons of water. Be careful not to overwork the dough when stirring.

Transfer the dough to a lightly floured surface and, using your hands, firmly form a ball. Cut the ball in half and form the two halves into balls. Flatten them each into a disc, then tightly wrap each disc in plastic wrap and chill for at least an hour.

Once chilled, transfer one disc to a floured surface and allow to sit for 5 minutes. Roll it out with a lightly floured rolling pin until approximately 12 inches in diameter. Carefully roll the crust back over the rolling pin and transfer to a ceramic or glass 9-inch pie plate, trying not to stretch it. Using your knuckles, pinch the dough to flute the edges. Brush the crust with egg white and chill again for 15 minutes before adding your filling. This will help your pie avoid having a soggy bottom!

If you're making Pumpkin Pie or Pecan Pie (page 126 or 129), you'll need to blind bake your crust before you fill it. To do so, preheat the oven to 400°F and using a fork, poke a few holes in the bottom of the crust. Carefully line the inside and top edge of the crust with parchment paper or heavy-duty aluminum foil. Fill with pie weights or dried beans. Bake for 15 minutes. Remove from the oven and carefully remove the foil and weights. Bake for another 10 minutes, or until golden. To avoid the edges from getting too brown when you bake the filled pie, use a pie shield (or create one out of foil).

If you're making a double-crust pie (one with a top crust), fill the pie, then remove the second dough disc from the refrigerator and roll it out like you did with the bottom crust. This is where the fun begins—you have so many options for the top! You can place the full crust on top and cut slits or a design in it to vent the pie, or you can do a lattice top (cut the dough into 12 strips, lay 7 strips over the top, and then weave the other 5 strips through), or even utilize cookie cutters to cut out a bunch of shapes and place them on top of a simple top crust. If you choose this last method, please note that you'll likely need to double this recipe, as it takes more dough to do that.

Scan for Video!

MIXED BERRY PIE

I t's my personal opinion that berries taste best when they join forces. Their flavors are all unique but work together in such a delicious way, and I find that to be particularly true with this pie. If you disagree, you can of course simply use 7 cups of your favorite berry. Given the juicy nature of these fruits, I like to precook them and prepare the filling before adding it to the crust to ensure the final product is thick, not runny.

Makes one 10-inch pie

2 cups fresh or frozen blueberries

2 cups fresh or frozen raspberries

2 cups fresh or frozen strawberries, hulled and quartered

1 cup fresh or frozen blackberries

1 cup sugar

¼ cup cornstarch

½ teaspoon salt

1 teaspoon ground cinnamon

1 tablespoon fresh lemon juice

2 tablespoons unsalted butter, cold and cubed

1 teaspoon pure vanilla extract

1 Perfect Piecrust (page 119), chilled in the pie tin

1 egg white, lightly beaten

Coarse sugar for sprinkling, optional

Preheat the oven to 400°F. Place a foil-lined, empty baking sheet on the middle rack.

In a Dutch oven, combine the blueberries, raspberries, strawberries, and blackberries. Add the sugar, cornstarch, salt, cinnamon, ⅓ cup water (eliminate if using frozen berries), and lemon juice and toss to coat the berries. Over medium heat, slowly bring the water to a boil, stirring regularly. Boil for 3 to 5 minutes, until thick. Remove from the heat and stir in the butter and vanilla extract. Allow to cool for 10 minutes before pouring the filling into the piecrust. Top with your second piecrust in the fashion of your choice (I created a lattice with cutouts for the photo). Brush the top with egg white, and if desired, sprinkle with coarse sugar.

Place on the preheated baking sheet to catch any drips and bake for 10 minutes. Reduce the temperature to 350°F and bake for another 40 to 45 minutes, until golden brown and bubbling. Check at 25 minutes and add a pie shield (or create your own out of foil) if the edges are getting too brown. Allow the pie to cool completely (for at least 2 hours) on a wire rack.

Once cool, slice it up, top with ice cream, and enjoy! Store leftovers covered in the refrigerator for up to 4 days.

APPLE PIE

Turns out a little sour cream is a welcome addition to the classic apple pie. If these apples were pasta, they'd be al dente—fully cooked but not devoid of texture—and enveloped in a perfectly sweet filling. Bye, bye, Miss American Pie!

Makes one 10-inch pie

4–5 large Honeycrisp apples (about 3 pounds), peeled, cored, and thinly sliced

¾ cup packed light brown sugar

¼ cup all-purpose flour

1 tablespoon cornstarch

½ teaspoon table salt

2 teaspoons ground cinnamon

3 tablespoons sour cream

1 tablespoon fresh lemon juice

1 teaspoon pure vanilla extract

1 Perfect Piecrust (page 119), chilled in the pie tin

2 tablespoons unsalted butter, cold and cubed

1 egg white, lightly beaten

Coarse sugar for sprinkling, optional

Vanilla ice cream for serving

Preheat the oven to 400°F. Place a foil-lined, empty baking sheet on the middle rack.

In a large bowl, combine the apple slices, brown sugar, flour, cornstarch, salt, cinnamon, sour cream, lemon juice, and vanilla extract. Toss together until well combined and the apples are all coated. Pour into a chilled, unbaked piecrust. Evenly distribute the cubes of butter around the top and gently press them into the filling. Top with your second piecrust in the fashion of your choice. Brush the top with egg white, and if desired, sprinkle with coarse sugar.

Place on the preheated baking sheet to catch any drips and bake for 10 minutes. Reduce the temperature to 350°F and bake for another 45 to 50 minutes, until golden brown and bubbling. Check at 25 minutes and add a pie shield (or create one out of foil) if the edges are getting too brown. Allow the pie to cool completely (for at least 2 hours) on a wire rack.

Once cool, slice and serve! Store leftovers covered in the refrigerator for up to 4 days.

PUMPKIN PIE

❦

Pumpkin has become as much a part of autumn as falling leaves. The flavor permeates everything from lattes to pasta, but I wouldn't want it any other way. Pumpkin is a rich, filling fruit, and the perfect pumpkin pie is a necessity for every kitchen. While there's rarely much variation from recipe to recipe on this classic, I tinkered with the sugars and spices to get the flavor I love so much in this pie. Using only brown sugar and a little extra cinnamon was the key, but if there's a flavor profile you're seeking, tinker away!

Makes one 10-inch pie

1 Perfect Piecrust (page 119), chilled in the pie tin

1 (15-ounce) can 100 percent pure pumpkin puree

3 large eggs

1½ cups packed light brown sugar

1 tablespoon plus 1 teaspoon cornstarch

½ teaspoon table salt

2 teaspoons ground cinnamon

½ teaspoon ground nutmeg

½ teaspoon ground ginger

¼ teaspoon ground cloves

1¼ cups evaporated milk

1 teaspoon pure vanilla extract

Crème de la Cloud (page 135)

Preheat the oven to 400°F. Place a foil-lined, empty baking sheet on the middle rack.

Blind bake the piecrust, as described on page 120.

While the crust bakes, make the filling. In a large mixing bowl, whisk together the pumpkin, eggs, and brown sugar. Add the cornstarch, salt, cinnamon, nutmeg, ginger, cloves, evaporated milk, and vanilla extract. Whisk vigorously until well combined.

After you remove the piecrust from the oven, reduce the oven temperature to 375°F.

Allow the crust to cool for 10 minutes, then pour the filling into the warm crust and distribute it evenly. Place on the preheated baking sheet to catch any drips and bake for 55 to 60 minutes, until most of the custard is set, but the very center still has a tiny jiggle to it. Check at 30 minutes and add a pie shield (or create one out of foil) if the

edges are getting too brown. Remove and allow to cool completely (for at least 2 hours) on a wire rack.

Once cool, slice up the pie and top each serving with a dollop of Crème de la Cloud! Store leftovers covered in the refrigerator for up to 4 days.

PECAN PIE

A southern tradition if there ever was one. I remember picking pecans as a little girl on my aunt Mittie Lou's farm in Texarkana, and pecan pie has been a staple at every Cowan Thanksgiving dinner. No matter how full you are after the big meal, there's always room for a little slice of toasted pecan heaven.

Makes one 10-inch pie

1 Perfect Piecrust (page 119), chilled in the pie tin

3 large eggs, beaten

½ cup light corn syrup

1 cup packed light brown sugar

½ teaspoon table salt

4 tablespoons (½ stick) unsalted butter, melted and cooled

2 teaspoons pure vanilla extract

1½ cups pecan pieces

Cinnamon-Infused Whipped Cream (page 132)

Preheat the oven to 400°F. Place a foil-lined, empty baking sheet on the middle rack.

Blind bake the piecrust, as described on page 120.

While the crust bakes, make the filling. In a large mixing bowl, beat the eggs and then whisk in the corn syrup, brown sugar, and salt. Whisk in the butter and vanilla extract until well combined. Stir in the pecan pieces.

After you remove the piecrust from the oven, reduce the oven temperature to 375°F.

Allow the crust to cool for 10 minutes, then pour the filling into the warm crust and distribute it evenly. Place on the preheated baking sheet to catch any drips and bake for 40 to 45 minutes, until the top is set and the pecans are a deep, rich brown. Check at 20 minutes and add a pie shield (or make one out of foil) if the edges are getting too brown. Allow the pie to cool completely (for at least 2 hours) on a wire rack.

Once cool, top each slice with a dollop of Cinnamon-Infused Whipped Cream, and dig in! Store leftovers covered in the refrigerator for up to 4 days.

BUTTERSCOTCH PUDDING
~with~
HOMEMADE WHIPPED CREAM

While I've spent a lifetime loving butterscotch pudding, I had never made it until 2014. I was hosting the Milk Jar holiday party at my home and wanted to make something really special for dessert. I decided that individual servings of homemade butterscotch pudding topped with whipped cream and dark chocolate Crispearls was the perfect choice. It felt special and just decadent enough. I'm not sure why, but I was a little nervous to make butterscotch pudding from scratch, but it was actually much easier than I thought it would be. The key is to take it slow and whisk constantly and thoroughly—you're going to get an arm workout—but you'll have the most delicious treat to share with your friends and family!

Makes 6 to 8 servings

2½ cups whole milk

1 cup heavy cream

6 tablespoons unsalted butter

1¼ cups packed light brown sugar

3 egg yolks

¼ cup cornstarch

½ teaspoon table salt

1½ teaspoons pure vanilla extract

Homemade Whipped Cream (recipe follows)

Crispearls (or substitue Nestlé Buncha Crunch clusters), for topping

In a Dutch oven over medium heat, combine the milk and heavy cream and bring to a simmer, stirring regularly. Remove from the heat immediately after it reaches a simmer and set aside. In a large skillet, melt the butter over medium-high heat. Add the brown sugar and increase the heat slightly. Stirring constantly, cook for 5 to 7 minutes to caramelize the mixture. When it's ready, you'll be able to smell that signature caramel fragrance.

Whisking constantly, gradually add the brown sugar mixture to the hot milk mixture. The brown sugar mixture will drop in slightly clumpy, so whisk thoroughly to break down the brown sugar, making sure it fully incorporates into the milk before adding more.

Put the egg yolks in a medium bowl and whisk lightly. Whisking constantly, slowly add half of the hot milk mixture. Whisk in the cornstarch and salt until dissolved. Whisk this mixture back into the remaining hot milk mixture in the Dutch oven. Whisking constantly, cook over medium-high heat until thick and just boiling. Once your whisk is leaving trail marks, remove from the heat and whisk in the vanilla extract. Pour the pudding into 6 to 8 ramekins and chill, uncovered, for at least 3 hours or even overnight.

Serve chilled and topped with Homemade Whipped Cream and Crispearls, which can be purchased online. In a pinch, you could substitute Nestlé Buncha Crunch clusters.

Store in the refrigerator for up to 3 days.

HOMEMADE WHIPPED CREAM

Makes 2 cups

1 cup heavy cream, cold

2 tablespoons powdered sugar

1 teaspoon pure vanilla extract

Using a hand mixer or a stand mixer with the whisk attachment, whip the heavy cream, powdered sugar, and vanilla extract on medium-high speed until medium-stiff peaks form, 4 to 5 minutes. Medium-stiff means your peaks will be stiff enough to hold their shape but will curl over at the top.

Serve immediately or cover tightly and refrigerate for up to 24 hours.

➤ RECIPE ALTERNATIVE: For a deliciously spicy treat, make my Cinnamon-Infused Whipped Cream by adding 1 teaspoon ground cinnamon.

CHOCOLATE PUDDING
~with~
CRÈME DE LA CLOUD

Mom made pudding from time to time and even though it was from a box, it felt so decadent and special because she always put it in these magically beautiful dishes that had pedestals! FANCY. As I was preparing to write this book, my first call was to my mom to make sure she shipped THE dishes to me. As you can see, beauty is in the eye of the beholder, but I still got that little twinkle of excitement as I transferred the pudding into them for the photos. While this pudding is delicious even if you just dip your finger in the pot, I highly recommend you serve it in little bowls that make YOU feel fancy.

Makes 6 to 8 servings

1 cup sugar

½ cup natural unsweetened cocoa powder

¼ cup cornstarch

½ teaspoon table salt

2½ cups whole milk

1½ cups heavy cream

1.45-ounce bar of dark chocolate, chopped

2 tablespoons unsalted butter

2 teaspoons pure vanilla extract

Homemade Crème de la Cloud (recipe follows)

In a Dutch oven, combine the sugar, cocoa powder, cornstarch, and salt. Over medium heat, add the milk, heavy cream, and chocolate and bring to a simmer, whisking regularly. Keep the heat on the lower side and take it slow to avoid burning the milk. Once the mixture reaches a simmer, whisk constantly and cook for 2 minutes. Remove from the heat and whisk in the butter and vanilla extract.

Pour into 6 to 8 beautiful dishes of your choosing (might I recommend ones with pedestals?) and chill, uncovered, for at least 3 hours or even overnight.

Serve chilled and topped with homemade Crème de la Cloud, and revel in your fanciness.

Store in the refrigerator for up to 3 days.

CRÈME DE LA CLOUD

In the Cowan home, we tended to prefer a thicker, sweeter commercially available dessert topping over homemade whipped cream, so I spent a long time nailing this recipe. It reminds everyone right away of the beloved big blue tub but is completely homemade. Use it to top pretty much anything or just eat it with a spoon! Note: It's all about the timing with this one, so keep your timer handy.

Makes 4 cups

1½ teaspoons powdered gelatin	1 tablespoon pure vanilla extract
2 tablespoons ice water	¼ cup water
¼ cup whole milk, cold	⅓ cup light corn syrup
3 tablespoons powdered milk	¾ cup sugar
2 tablespoons powdered sugar	½ teaspoon salt
	1¾ cups heavy cream, cold

In a small bowl, whisk together the gelatin and ice water. Set aside.

In another small bowl, whisk together the milk, powdered milk, powdered sugar, and vanilla extract. Set aside.

In a small saucepan, whisk together the water, corn syrup, sugar, and salt. Over medium heat and whisking regularly, bring to a rolling boil and cook for 5 minutes, creating a mixture that looks like simple syrup. Turn off the heat and pour the boiling mixture into the metal bowl of a stand mixer with the whisk attachment. Let cool for 3 minutes and then add the gelatin mixture. Mix on medium speed for 6 to 8 minutes, until cool and white in color. With the mixer still running, gradually add the milk mixture, allowing it to incorporate before adding more. Once the mixture is fully combined, stop the mixer, remove the whisk from the mixture, cover, and allow to sit for 2 hours.

With the mixer running on low speed, slowly add the heavy cream. Turn the speed up to high and mix until you get stiff peaks, approximately 10 minutes.

Serve immediately or cover tightly and refrigerate for up to 3 days. You can also freeze for up to a month.

BANANA SPLIT PUPPY CHOW

One of my favorite things about baking is putting a new twist on something classic. A great deal of my inspiration for cookie flavors comes from that idea, but this recipe flips the script. During a visit with my cousin, we were brainstorming about fun new things to make inspired by my cookie flavors instead. This crowd-pleasing treat is a super fun and easy addition to your next game night or gathering. And, don't worry—freeze-dried strawberries are easy to find! Check online for local stores that carry them.

Serves 8 to 10

1 cup semisweet chocolate chips	1¼ cups freeze-dried strawberries
1 cup butterscotch chips	1¼ cups walnut pieces
6 cups Rice Chex	1 cup powdered sugar
1 teaspoon pure banana extract	

In a medium saucepan, melt together the chocolate and butterscotch chips over low heat, stirring regularly. Slow and steady is the name of the game here so the chocolate doesn't burn and get clumpy. (Alternatively, melt your chocolate in a heat-proof bowl in the microwave: see page 143.)

In a large mixing bowl, add 3 cups of the Rice Chex. Pour half of the melted chocolate mixture over the cereal and gently stir until all of the cereal is fully coated. Drizzle ½ teaspoon of the banana extract over the coated cereal and gently stir to equally disperse. Repeat with the remaining cereal, melted chocolate mixture, and banana extract, making sure all of the cereal is completely coated. Fold in the freeze-dried strawberries and walnuts and gently stir until they are equally distributed. Sprinkle the powdered sugar over the top and stir until everything is coated in powdered sugar and the individual pieces of the snack mix start to separate.

Serve in a cute bowl or store in an airtight container for up to 5 days.

HOOSIER HAYSTACKS

❦

Family traditions were a very big part of my upbringing, and as I've grown up, I have found great joy in creating my own traditions. I have also realized that even the simplest of circumstances can present the chance to start one. As a freshman at Indiana University (go Hoosiers!), I created my very first personal tradition. After a test one day, I went to get a snack and discovered this crunchy, peanut butter-y concoction they had in the library cafeteria. I found myself thinking about this delicious little treat for days and decided that I would make it my post-test tradition. So began years of visits to the library cafeteria to celebrate (or perhaps eat my feelings) after a test. After I graduated and moved to Los Angeles, I couldn't find any treats like it, so I set out to recreate it. A couple tips: natural peanut butters without sugars do not work as well here, so stick with the classics. And the flake size and crunchy texture of Special K cereal, specifically, impacts the final product. Here's to simple pleasures and special moments!

Makes 12 to 15 treats, depending on scoop size

1 cup sugar

1 cup light corn syrup

1½ teaspoons pure vanilla extract

¼ teaspoon table salt

1⅓ cups creamy peanut butter

5 cups Special K cereal

In a Dutch oven over medium-low heat, heat the sugar, light corn syrup, vanilla extract, and salt, stirring constantly until the sugar is dissolved. Take it slow, as heating the sugar and syrup too quickly will cause your treats to get hard instead of chewy. Add the peanut butter and stir until fully melted and combined. Remove the pot from the heat and fold in the cereal. Gently stir until all of the cereal is fully coated in the peanut butter mixture. If you use a wooden spoon, spray a little nonstick spray on it to keep your treats from sticking.

Using an ice cream scoop or large spoon, scoop up small amounts of the mixture while still warm and place each dollop on parchment paper until cool, approximately 15 minutes.

Serve and enjoy or store in an airtight container for up to 4 days.

PB&J KRISPY TREATS

R ice Krispy treats were one of the first things I learned how to make on my own when I was a kid, and I just love the simplicity of them. As I have a tendency to do, I decided to complicate things one day and threw some peanut butter in the pot. WHOA. That took it up a notch. Then another day, I was feeling saucy and thought of adding raspberry preserves to the mix. DOUBLE WHOA. I love this sweet take on a classic PB&J sandwich so much, and it's a total crowd-pleaser! I'm excited for you to make these easy treats—you don't even have to cut off the crusts!

 *Serves 8 to 10*

3 tablespoons unsalted butter

1 (10-ounce) bag of marshmallows (I'm a Jet-Puffed girl)

⅔ cup creamy peanut butter

6 cups Rice Krispies cereal

½ cup raspberry preserves

In a Dutch oven, melt the butter over low heat. Add the marshmallows and, using a rubber spatula, stir until completely melted. Stir in the peanut butter until incorporated. Remove from the heat and add the Rice Krispies. Stir until fully combined.

Simultaneously, in a small saucepan, warm the raspberry preserves on low heat to thin them out.

Using a greased spoon or wax paper, spread half the Rice Krispies mixture into an 8-inch square pan. Drizzle half of the preserves over that. Repeat with the remaining Rice Krispies mixture and preserves to create a two-layered treat.

Allow to cool for about 10 to 15 minutes. Cut and serve with a cold glass of milk!

If these treats last more than the day, cover and store at room temperature for up to 4 days.

CHOCOLATE-COVERED PRETZELS

S o. Much. Fun! And so easy. The options are endless. Perfect little salty-sweet treat. This isn't a recipe so much as a creative license—go wild and have a great time. The key is to have a good, thick coating of chocolate so the ratio of chocolate to pretzel is satisfying in each bite.

Makes about 30 pieces

2 (12-ounce) bags chocolate chips (I prefer semisweet)

1 (12-ounce) bag pretzel rods

OPTIONAL GARNISHES:

Colored nonpareils

Chopped nuts

Sprinkles

Sanding sugars

Line a baking sheet with parchment paper.

In a medium saucepan, melt the chocolate chips on low heat, stirring regularly. Slow and steady is the name of the game here so the chocolate doesn't burn and get clumpy. Once the chocolate is smooth, turn off the heat.

Dip one end of a pretzel rod into the chocolate, and, using a spoon, cover all but the end you're holding in chocolate, spinning the rod for even coverage. Do this twice to ensure a nice, thick coating. Holding the rod over the saucepan, spin it a couple times, allowing the excess chocolate to fall back into the pan. Sprinkle with nonpareils or any of the other decorations you choose and then lay the pretzel rod flat on the parchment paper. Repeat to your heart's content!

Store in an airtight container at room temperature for up to 2 weeks.

* NOTE: You can also melt your chocolate chips in the microwave! In a microwave safe bowl, heat for 30 seconds then stir. Repeat as needed, stirring each time, until melted.

BANANA PUDDING

—with—

VANILLA WAFER COOKIES

As young kids, my brother, Todd, and I would often spend the night at my grandmother's house, and I remember her making delicious banana pudding. One night when I was five years old, I was in the bathroom, and Earl (my grandfather who only had one eye—a story for another time) opened the door and said in his deadpan way, "nanner puddin's ready." I recall this as if it was yesterday and still giggle at the memory. When I take a bite of this pudding and close my eyes, I'm right back at Grannie's house playing beats on my Casio keyboard or watching a very loud TV, sharing a bowl of nanner puddin' with Todd. While I like serving puddings individually, you can also make a big bowl of it. Get creative and have fun with the layering of bananas, wafers, and pudding.

And side note: if you're feeling pressed for time, using the classic store-bought Nilla Wafers like Grannie did is 100 percent A-OK.

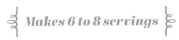

Makes 6 to 8 servings

4 tablespoons all-purpose flour

1 cup sugar

½ cup packed light brown sugar

½ teaspoon table salt

3 extra-large egg yolks

1½ cups whole milk

1½ cups heavy cream

2 medium overripe bananas, mashed into pulp

2 teaspoons pure vanilla extract

Vanilla Wafer Cookies (recipe follows), plus a few crushed to sprinkle on top for garnish

2–3 just-ripe bananas, sliced

In a large saucepan, whisk together the flour, sugar, brown sugar, and salt.

In a medium bowl, lightly beat the egg yolks. Add the milk and heavy cream and stir. Pour into the saucepan and whisk to combine with the dry ingredients. Stir in the banana pulp and cook over medium heat, whisking regularly. Keep the heat on

Scan for Video!

the lower side and take it slow to avoid burning the milk. Once it reaches a simmer, whisk constantly and cook for 2 to 3 minutes, until the pudding mixture thickens and your whisk is leaving trail marks. Remove from the heat and whisk in the vanilla extract.

To layer your puddings, place 2 or 3 wafers on the bottom of each dish and top with a few banana slices. Pour the pudding on top of that. Line the edge of the dish with wafers. Repeat in as many dishes as you want, and chill, uncovered, for at least 3 hours or even overnight. Before serving, place 2 slices of banana and some wafer crumbs on top.

Store in the refrigerator for up to 3 days.

VANILLA WAFER COOKIES

Makes 50 to 55 cookies

½ cup (1 stick) unsalted butter, softened

½ cup powdered sugar

¼ cup sugar

1 tablespoon packed light brown sugar

¼ cup whole milk, cold

2 teaspoons pure vanilla extract

1¼ cups all-purpose flour

½ teaspoon salt

Preheat the oven to 350°F.

In a medium bowl or the bowl of a stand mixer with the paddle attachment, cream the butter, powdered sugar, sugar, and brown sugar. Add the milk and vanilla extract and mix until fully combined. Mix in the flour and salt until just combined.

Line two baking sheets with parchment paper. Transfer the batter to a piping bag with a 1A tip and pipe 1-inch circles. If you don't have a piping bag and tip, you can use a large plastic storage bag and cut the corner off; you might just need to shape the circles of batter a bit with your fingers. Bake on the middle and lower racks of the oven until the tops are a light golden brown, 20 to 22 minutes, spinning each pan 180 degrees and swapping their positions halfway through.

Let the cookies cool completely. Store in an airtight container and keep at room temperature for up to 4 days or freeze for up to a month.

MARSHMALLOWS

Marshmallows were always a treat that fascinated me. How do they make them so bouncy? And what are they exactly (aside from the mechanism for an intense game of "chubby bunny," of course)? I really couldn't wrap my head around it, so that, of course, meant I had to try to make some! They are surprisingly easy and so much fun to make, and watching them come together is reminiscent of watching taffy being pulled in an old candy shop window. Mesmerizing! While precision is key, one thing you *can* play with is the color! I added two drops of red food coloring to the ones pictured to get that beautiful light pink. Note: It's all about the timing with this one, so keep your stopwatch handy.

Makes about 75 to 80 marshmallows

¼ cup powdered sugar	1½ cups sugar
¼ cup cornstarch	1 cup light corn syrup
3 (¼-ounce) packages unflavored gelatin	¼ teaspoon table salt
1 cup ice water	1½ teaspoons pure vanilla extract

In a small bowl, whisk together the powdered sugar and cornstarch.

Lightly spray a 13 by 9-inch pan with nonstick spray, then add the powdered sugar mixture. Move the mixture around in the pan until the bottom and sides are coated, then return the excess to the bowl for later use.

In the bowl of a stand mixer with the whisk attachment, combine the gelatin and ½ cup of the ice water. Set aside.

In a small saucepan, whisk together the remaining ½ cup of ice water, the sugar, corn syrup, and salt. Cover and cook over medium-high heat for 4 minutes. Uncover, stir, and continue cooking for 8 minutes. Remove from the heat.

With the mixer on low speed, slowly pour the sugar mixture down the side of the stand mixer bowl into the gelatin. Once all of the sugar mixture has been added, turn the

mixer up to high and let mix for 15 minutes, or until the mixture is very thick and looks like taffy being pulled. Add the vanilla extract around minute 14.

Pour the marshmallow mixture into the prepared pan, using a lightly greased spoon or spatula to spread it out. Dust the top lightly with the powdered sugar mixture and reserve the rest for later. Cover and allow to sit for at least 4 hours or up to overnight.

Turn the marshmallows out onto a cutting board and cut to desired size using a knife or pizza wheel coated in the reserved powdered sugar mixture. Lightly dust the sides of each treat using the remaining powdered sugar mixture, and voila! You've got marshmallows!

Store in an airtight container at room temperature for up to 2 weeks.

CHOCOLATE FUDGE

Fudge is a delightful treat that has a very special place in my heart. I grew up visiting family friends in the Upper Peninsula of Michigan each summer, and one of my favorite things we did was go to Mackinac Island for the day. As we'd walk around, I was always captivated by the fudge makers in the shop windows forming their treats on the marble slabs (something I would later learn is what made Mackinac fudge special). We never left without a big slice to nibble on for the rest of our trip. Then, at age sixteen, I would find my first gainful employment at a candy shop in the local mall called Arlene's Corner Sweet Shoppe, where fudge was a big part of the business. While we didn't prepare it on marble slabs at Arlene's, I still felt like I'd really made it to the big leagues.

Makes 8 to 10 servings

4 cups sugar

1 cup whole milk

1 teaspoon pure vanilla extract

1 cup (2 sticks) unsalted butter, cubed

1½ cups mini marshmallows

2 (12-ounce) bags chocolate chips (I prefer semisweet)

½ bar (2 ounces) unsweetened baking chocolate, chopped

1 cup chopped walnuts, optional

Line a 1-pound bread pan with parchment paper.

In a large saucepan, whisk together the sugar, milk, and vanilla. Add the butter, and over medium-low heat, bring to a boil, whisking regularly. Keep the heat on the lower side and take it slow to avoid burning the milk. Once it reaches a boil, whisk constantly and cook for 2 minutes, allowing it to thicken slightly. Remove from the heat and stir in the marshmallows. Then add the chopped chocolate and chocolate chips a little at a time, stirring thoroughly after each addition. If you'd like to, add the walnuts, and then pour the fudge mixture into the bread pan. Chill until firm, approximately 20 minutes. Slice, and enjoy!

Store in an airtight container at room temperature for up to 7 days.

TAPIOCA PUDDING

I'm very big on the texture of food, so I always avoided tapioca pudding because of the gelatinous nature of the pearls. Why mess with it when there were so many other flavors of pudding that I enjoyed? My husband, Adam, loves tapioca pudding, so I eventually tried it. The things we do for love, right? Needless to say, I'd been missing out! When prepared correctly, the tapioca pearls enhance the pudding, as opposed to sticking out like the sore thumbs I always thought them to be. Call me extra, but I love topping each serving with Cinnamon-Infused Whipped Cream, fresh raspberries, and chocolate shavings. This adds a little complexity and almost makes it too pretty to eat . . . almost.

Makes 6 to 8 servings

¾ cup large (#40) tapioca pearls

2 cups whole milk

1 cup heavy cream

2 extra-large eggs

¼ cup sugar

¼ cup packed light brown sugar

½ teaspoon salt

2 teaspoons pure vanilla extract

Cinnamon-Infused Whipped Cream (see page 132)

Cover the tapioca pearls with water, soak for 2 hours, then drain.

In a large saucepan, whisk together the milk, cream, eggs, sugar, brown sugar, and salt. Stir in the tapioca pearls. Over medium-low heat and stirring constantly, bring the mixture to a simmer and cook for 2 to 3 minutes, until it begins to thicken. Remove from the heat and stir in the vanilla extract. Let cool 5 minutes.

Pour into 6 to 8 beautiful dishes and chill, uncovered, for at least 3 hours or overnight.

Serve cold, topped with cinnamon-infused whipped cream.

Store covered in the refrigerator for up to 3 days.

SOUR CREAM COFFEE CAKE

My aunt and uncle used to eat so much coffee cake for breakfast that they began affectionately dubbing it "dog food" because they ate the same thing every morning and never tired of it. I'm quite certain they are solely responsible for the success of Entenmann's. As is the case with a lot of my recipes, I was excited to develop my own twist on a classic that is important to my family. This coffee cake is delicious enough to delight and elegant enough to impress. I love to make it for brunch with friends or just for a relaxing Saturday morning. While you can use a standard cake pan, I bake mine in a classic Bundt pan to give it that extra charm. And, if you want to eat it every morning, I can't say I'd blame you.

Makes one Bundt cake

FOR THE CAKE:

¾ cup (1½ sticks) unsalted butter, room temperature, plus more for the pan

2½ cups all-purpose flour, plus more for the pan

1 teaspoon baking powder

1 teaspoon baking soda

½ teaspoon table salt

½ cup sugar

1 cup packed light brown sugar

3 extra-large eggs, cold

1½ teaspoons pure vanilla extract

1¼ cups sour cream

FOR THE STREUSEL:

½ cup all-purpose flour

1½ teaspoons ground cinnamon

¼ teaspoon table salt

¼ cup packed light brown sugar

3 tablespoons unsalted butter, cold and cubed

FOR THE GLAZE:

½ cup powdered sugar

2 tablespoons real maple syrup

1 teaspoon pure vanilla extract

1 teaspoon pure almond extract

Preheat the oven to 350°F. Grease and flour a 12-cup Bundt pan.

TO MAKE THE CAKE: In a medium bowl, sift together the flour, baking powder, baking soda, and salt. Set aside.

In a large mixing bowl with a wooden spoon or the bowl of a stand mixer with the paddle attachment, cream the butter, sugar, and brown sugar, 3 to 4 minutes. Mix in the eggs one at a time, on low speed, until just combined. Add the vanilla extract and sour cream and mix until just incorporated, approximately 1 minute. Add the flour mixture and mix on low speed until just combined. Scrape down the sides of the bowl and stir to make sure everything is combined.

TO MAKE THE STREUSEL: In a small bowl, combine the flour, cinnamon, salt, brown sugar, and butter. Using your fingers, pinch the ingredients all together until they form a crumble.

Pour half of the batter into the prepared pan and spread it out with a spoon so it's evenly distributed. Sprinkle half of the streusel evenly on top. Pour the rest of the batter in the pan, spread it out, and then top with the remaining streusel. Bake for 50 to 55 minutes, until a toothpick inserted in the top of the cake comes out clean.

Let cool on a wire rack for 30 to 45 minutes. Place a platter upside down on top of the pan and quickly flip it over. Carefully lift the pan and unmold the cake.

TO MAKE THE GLAZE: In a small bowl, whisk together the powdered sugar, maple syrup, and vanilla and almond extracts to create a runny glaze. If needed, you can add a couple drops of water. Drizzle as much glaze as you'd like over the cake. Let it sit for 15 minutes while you brew a pot of coffee, then slice and serve!

Store covered at room temperature for up to 4 days or freeze for up to 1 month.

Scan for Tunes!

COURTNEY COWAN

PUMPKIN BREAD

While studies show that sensory memories last only a short time, I'm guessing they've never studied pumpkin bread and its effects on a person's brain. The taste of pumpkin bread immediately transports me back to a fall day in Westfield, Indiana, sitting on a bale of hay at an autumn festival, devouring a slice of perfectly moist pumpkin bread. I can feel the cool breeze on my face and see the brightly colored leaves, and there's nothing quite like it. The beauty of making a loaf yourself is that you don't have to wait for pumpkin-spice season to roll around—go wild and make it in the middle of the summer if you want!

Makes one 1-pound loaf

¾ cup (1½ sticks) unsalted butter, softened, plus more for the pan

2 cups all-purpose flour, plus more for the pan

½ teaspoon table salt

1 teaspoon baking soda

½ teaspoon baking powder

1 teaspoon ground cloves

1 teaspoon ground cinnamon

1 teaspoon ground nutmeg

1 cup sugar

1 cup packed light brown sugar

2 extra-large eggs

1 teaspoon pure vanilla extract

1 (15-ounce) can 100-percent pure pumpkin puree

Preheat the oven to 325°F.

Generously grease a 1-pound loaf pan with butter and dust with flour. Alternatively, cut parchment paper to line the pan.

In a medium bowl, combine the flour, salt, baking soda, baking powder, cloves, cinnamon, and nutmeg. Whisk until well mixed and set aside.

In a large mixing bowl with a wooden spoon or the bowl of a stand mixer with the paddle attachment, cream the butter, sugar, and brown sugar. Add the eggs one at a time, beating well after each addition. Continue beating for a few minutes, until the mixture is very light and fluffy. Beat in the vanilla extract and pumpkin. It might look grainy and lumpy at this point—don't worry!

Add the flour mixture and mix on medium-low speed until combined.

Pour the batter into the prepared pan and bake on the middle rack for 65 to 75 minutes, until a toothpick inserted into the center comes out clean. Let the loaf cool in the pan for about 10 minutes, run a knife around the edges, then turn it onto a wire rack to cool completely. If using parchment paper, lift it out and place on the cooling rack.

Store at room temperature for up to 5 days or freeze for up to 1 month. After the first day, slice and toast it for that fresh-baked goodness.

*** NOTE:** If you prefer, you can divide the batter between two smaller loaf pans; just decrease the bake time to 55 to 65 minutes if you do.

MAMA'S CINNAMON ROLLS

Maybe it's the blood-sugar spike, but cinnamon rolls have always had a way of improving my mood. Whether they're from a fast-food joint or mom's own kitchen, they just hit the spot. These pinwheels of sweet yeast dough, loads of butter and cinnamon, smothered in icing are a bit of an undertaking but deliver the best payoff as they melt in your mouth and your worries momentarily melt away, too. While I love mine with a classic filling of raisins, the options run the gamut. You can add walnuts, pecans, almonds, chocolate chips, hazelnut spread—anything your heart desires! And, if you don't have a dough hook attachment, you can use the paddle or a hand mixer until you add the yeast, after which I recommend using your hands.

Makes 12 to 15 rolls

FOR THE ROLLS:

1 (¼-ounce) package rapid rise yeast

½ cup warm water

½ cup scalded milk

¼ cup sugar plus ¼ cup for the pan

⅓ cup unsalted butter plus 2 tablespoons for the pan

1 teaspoon table salt

1 extra-large egg

3¾ cups all-purpose flour, plus more for rising and rolling

FOR THE FILLING:

½ cup unsalted butter, melted

1 cup sugar

2 tablespoons plus 2 teaspoons ground cinnamon (or 3 tablespoons if you LOVE cinnamon)

¾ cup raisins, optional

FOR THE GLAZE:

4 tablespoons (½ stick) unsalted butter

2 cups powdered sugar

1 teaspoon pure vanilla extract

4–5 tablespoons hot water

TO MAKE THE ROLLS: In a small bowl, dissolve the yeast in the warm water. Set aside.

In a large mixing bowl with a wooden spoon or the bowl of a stand mixer with the dough hook attachment, beat the scalded milk, sugar, butter, salt, and egg on low speed until combined, approximately 1 minute. Add 2 cups of the flour and mix until smooth.

Pour in the yeast mixture and mix on low speed, gradually adding the remaining 1¾ cups flour and mixing until the dough is pulling away from the sides of the bowl. Transfer the dough to a lightly floured surface and knead for 5 to 10 minutes, until it is soft and elastic. Place the dough in a greased bowl, cover, and let rise until the dough doubles in size, 1 to 1½ hours.

Preheat the oven to 350°F.

To shape and fill the rolls: When doubled in size, punch down the dough to remove any bubbles that have formed. On a floured surface, roll out the dough into a 15 by 9-inch rectangle. Using a pastry brush, spread the melted butter all over the dough. In a small bowl, combine the sugar and cinnamon and sprinkle half of the mixture over the buttered dough, reserving the other half. Sprinkle the raisins evenly across, if using. Working from the long side, roll the dough into a log, pinching the seam and the ends to close. Using a serrated knife, cut into 12 to 15 pieces.

Coat the bottom of a 9 by 13-inch ceramic baking pan with butter and sprinkle with half of the remaining cinnamon sugar mixture. Place the rolls close together in the pan, and sprinkle the tops with the remaining cinnamon sugar. Cover with plastic wrap and allow to rise until the rolls double in size, approximately 45 minutes.

Bake for 30 minutes, or until lightly browned. Allow to cool for 20 to 30 minutes.

TO MAKE THE GLAZE: In a small bowl, beat together the butter, powdered sugar, and vanilla extract until combined. Whisk in the hot water. If a thinner glaze is desired, add another tablespoon of hot water. Pour the glaze over the rolls, distributing the glaze evenly.

Serve and enjoy the fruits of your labor!

Store covered at room temperature for up to 4 days or freeze for up to a month.

Scan for Video!

AUNT SUZ'S BANANA NUT BREAD

My aunt Suz has never met a stranger, and her generosity knows no bounds. This makes her holiday season very busy, as she bakes banana nut bread for everyone she knows. As a little girl, I watched her kitchen turn into a bread factory, with tin loaf pans cooling on every surface for days on end. It made an impression on me because it was the first time I had seen someone bake in bulk and realized that baking can be a great way to show someone you care. Whether you're making a single loaf for yourself or mini loaves to give away, this simply delicious recipe is one that will fill your home with an intoxicating fragrance and your heart with joy.

Makes one 1-pound loaf

6 tablespoons unsalted butter, softened, plus more for the pan

1½ cups all-purpose flour, plus more for the pan

1 cup sugar

2 extra-large eggs

1 teaspoon baking soda

3 tablespoons buttermilk

⅔ cup mashed banana (from about 2 bananas)

½ cup chopped pecans

Preheat the oven to 350°F.

Generously grease a 1-pound loaf pan with butter and dust with flour. Alternatively, cut parchment paper to line the pan.

In a large mixing bowl with a wooden spoon or the bowl of a stand mixer with the paddle attachment, beat the butter, sugar, and eggs on medium speed until creamy. Beat in the baking soda and buttermilk until just combined. Add the flour and mix until combined. Add the mashed banana and pecans and mix well, 1 to 2 minutes.

Transfer the batter into the prepared pan and bake on the middle rack for 35 to 40 minutes, until a toothpick inserted into the center comes out clean. Let the loaf cool in the pan for about 10 minutes, then turn it onto a wire rack to cool completely.

Store at room temperature for up to 5 days or freeze for up to 2 months. After the first day, slice and toast it for that fresh-baked goodness.

---

* NOTE: If you prefer, you can divide the batter between two smaller loaf pans; just decrease the bake time to 30 to 35 minutes if you do.

BLUEBERRY STREUSEL MUFFINS

So many mornings in the Cowan home were blessed with blueberry muffins. Even though they were from the box then, I remember getting so excited when the smell wafted up the stairs. I'd pick up my pace a little bit to make sure I got down there while they were still warm. Slice 'em in half and slather them with butter, and it was going to be a great day. This recipe is my grown-up spin, and while it calls for fresh blueberries, you can certainly use frozen when they are out of season.

Makes 12 muffins

FOR THE STREUSEL:

2 tablespoons sugar

2 tablespoons packed light brown sugar

1 tablespoon all-purpose flour

2 teaspoons vegetable oil

FOR THE MUFFINS:

2 cups all-purpose flour

1 teaspoon table salt

1½ teaspoons baking powder

½ cup (1 stick) unsalted butter, softened

½ cup sugar

½ cup packed light brown sugar

2 extra-large eggs

2 teaspoons pure vanilla extract

¾ cup whole milk

2 cups fresh blueberries

TO MAKE THE STREUSEL: In a small bowl, whisk together the sugar, brown sugar, and flour. Drizzle the vegetable oil into the bowl and use your fingers to work the ingredients all together until a sandy texture forms. Set aside.

TO MAKE THE MUFFINS: Preheat the oven to 350°F.

In a medium mixing bowl, whisk together the flour, salt, and baking powder.

In a large mixing bowl with a wooden spoon or the bowl of a stand mixer with the paddle attachment, cream together the butter, sugar, and brown sugar. Add the eggs, vanilla extract, and milk and mix until well combined. Pour this mixture into the dry ingredients and mix until just combined, approximately 1 minute. Be careful not to overmix. Fold in the blueberries.

Line a muffin tin with paper baking cups or spray the cups with nonstick baking spray. Using an ice cream scoop or large spoon, distribute the batter evenly between the 12 muffin cups. Top each with streusel.

Bake for 22 to 25 minutes, until golden brown around the edges and lightly browned on top; a toothpick inserted into the center should come out clean. Let them cool for a few minutes, then remove from the pan and slather with butter. Serve with a cold glass of milk!

Store in an airtight container at room temperature for up to 4 days or freeze for up to a month.

BACON CHEDDAR SCONES

I've long loved the idea of scones, but finding a good one out in the wild has proven difficult. They are often hard and dry and lacking in flavor. I spent many a morning tweaking this recipe until I finally created my perfect scone. I love the richness of adding bacon and cheese and serving them with a green salad, but when I'm looking for something a little sweeter, I substitute 1¼ cups of fresh berries and top each scone with a little turbinado sugar.

Makes 8 scones

1 pound bacon

4 ounces cheddar cheese, shredded (about 1 cup)

2 cups all-purpose flour, plus more for shaping the scones

½ cup sugar

2 tablespoons light brown sugar

½ teaspoon table salt

2 teaspoons baking powder

½ cup (1 stick) unsalted butter, frozen

¾ cup heavy cream, plus 2 tablespoons for brushing

1 extra-large egg

1½ teaspoons pure vanilla extract

Cook the bacon in a skillet until very crispy. While it cools, shred the cheese. When the bacon is cool enough, use your hands to crumble it into bits (you should have about 1 cup). Set the cheese and bacon aside.

In a large bowl, whisk together the flour, sugar, brown sugar, salt, and baking powder.

Grate the frozen butter using a box grater and add it to the flour mixture. Using your hands, work the butter in until the mixture is well combined and crumbly in texture.

Whisk ¾ cup of the heavy cream, the egg, and vanilla extract together in a small bowl. Drizzle over the flour and butter mixture, add the bacon crumbles and cheese, then stir together until combined.

Pour the dough onto a floured surface and work it into a ball. The dough will be a little sticky, so you may want to flour your hands, as well. Press into a disc about 8 inches across and 1 inch thick. Using a sharp knife, cut the dough into 8 wedges.

Brush the scones with the remaining 2 tablespoons heavy cream and refrigerate for 20 minutes.

While the scones are chilling, preheat the oven to 400°F.

Line a baking sheet with parchment paper and arrange the chilled scones on it.

Bake for 17 to 22 minutes, until golden brown around the edges and lightly browned on top. Allow to cool for a few minutes and then dig in!

Store in an airtight container at room temperature for up to 2 days or freeze for up to a month.

MRS. Z'S
CHOCOLATE CHOCOLATE CHIP
ZUCCHINI BREAD

Growing up next door to the Zaleski family is one of the greatest gifts life has given me. They welcomed us to our Indiana neighborhood on a snowy January day in 1985 and quickly became like family. Mrs. Z was cooking and baking all the time, and I remember vividly the day she brought over a few loaves of her zucchini bread for us. I'm sorry, did you say zucchini *bread*? I had never heard of such a thing and to take a bite and taste that it was chocolatey and sweet? Mind. Blown. This recipe is one of my favorite treats to bring to work or gatherings with friends.

Makes one 1-pound loaf

Butter for greasing the pan

2 cups all-purpose flour, plus more for dusting

3 extra-large eggs

2 cups sugar

1 cup vegetable oil

1 teaspoon table salt

1 teaspoon baking soda

2 teaspoons baking powder

2 teaspoons pure vanilla extract

1 cup whole wheat flour

4 tablespoons natural unsweetened cocoa powder

2 cups finely grated zucchini (from about 3 medium zucchini)

½ cup crushed pineapple, well drained

½ cup semisweet chocolate chips

⅓ cup walnut or pecan pieces, optional

Preheat the oven to 350°F.

Generously grease a 1-pound loaf pan with butter and dust with flour. Alternatively, cut parchment paper to line the pan.

In a large mixing bowl with a wooden spoon or a stand mixer with the paddle attachment, beat the eggs and sugar on medium speed until foamy, 3 to 4 minutes. Beat in the oil until the mixture is fluffy, 4 to 5 minutes. Add the salt, baking soda, baking powder, and vanilla extract and beat until well combined. Add the all-purpose and whole wheat flours, 1 cup at a time, mixing until each addition is incorporated before adding the next. Mix in the cocoa powder until well combined. Using a wooden spoon, stir in the zucchini, pineapple, chocolate chips, and nuts, if desired.

Pour the batter into the prepared pan and bake on the middle rack for 55 to 60 minutes, until a toothpick inserted into the center comes out clean. Let the loaf cool in the pan for about 10 minutes, then turn it onto a wire rack to cool completely.

Store at room temperature for up to 5 days or freeze for up to 1 month. After the first day, slice and toast it for that fresh-baked goodness.

* NOTE: If you prefer, you can divide the batter between two smaller loaf pans; just decrease the bake time to 50 minutes.

LEMON RICOTTA PANCAKES
~with~
BLUEBERRY COMPOTE

his is a decadent alternative to the classic pancake recipe, and it will definitely liven up a brunch or even the dreariest of midweek mornings. It may sound like a lot is going on in this recipe, but the flavors are delightfully balanced. The compote can be made up to three days in advance, stored in the refrigerator, and heated before serving.

Makes 8 to 10 pancakes, depending how big you make them

FOR THE COMPOTE:

2 cups fresh or frozen blueberries

3 tablespoons sugar

2 tablespoons water (reduce to 1 tablespoon if using frozen berries)

2 teaspoons fresh lemon juice

1½ teaspoons cornstarch

FOR THE PANCAKES:

1¼ cups all-purpose flour

3 tablespoons sugar

2 teaspoons baking powder

½ teaspoon baking soda

½ teaspoon table salt

1 cup ricotta cheese

1 extra-large egg

2 extra-large egg whites

½ cup fresh lemon juice

2 teaspoons grated lemon zest

1 teaspoon pure vanilla extract

1 tablespoon vegetable oil

TO MAKE THE COMPOTE: In a medium saucepan, combine the blueberries, sugar, and water. Bring to a boil over medium-high heat, stirring regularly. Reduce to a simmer and stir in the lemon juice and cornstarch until well combined. Continue to simmer and stir until the mixture thickens. Remove from the heat and cover to keep warm.

TO MAKE THE PANCAKES: In a large bowl, whisk together the flour, sugar, baking powder, baking soda, and salt.

In a medium bowl, whisk together the ricotta cheese, egg, egg whites, lemon juice, lemon zest, vanilla extract, and vegetable oil. Carefully fold the wet ingredients into the dry ingredients until the flour is fully combined. The batter will be thick, so be careful not to overmix.

Heat a skillet over medium heat and spray with nonstick cooking spray. Pour approximately ⅓ cup of batter per pancake and cook for 2 to 3 minutes on each side. When bubbles are forming on the top, your pancakes are ready to flip. Repeat until the batter is gone.

Serve hot, slathered with butter and topped with the warm blueberry compote. Good morning, indeed!

Store in airtight container in the refrigerator for up to 4 days or freeze for up to a month. Reheat in a 350°F oven for 5 to 8 minutes for the best "just-made" experience.

BANANA SPLIT WAFFLES

ω

So easy, slightly decadent, and oh so beautiful, the wrong side of the bed won't be an option on mornings that start with these waffles. If you aren't in the mood for something so sweet, feel free to omit the banana extract, chocolate chips, butterscotch chips, and walnuts for a delicious, straightforward classic.

 *Makes approximately 4 Belgian-style waffles*

2 cups all-purpose flour

1 tablespoon sugar

1 tablespoon baking powder

½ teaspoon table salt

1¾ cups buttermilk

2 extra-large eggs

½ teaspoon pure vanilla extract

1 teaspoon pure banana extract

½ cup unsalted butter, melted, plus pats of butter for serving

¼ cup semisweet chocolate chips

¼ cup butterscotch chips

¼ cup chopped walnut pieces, plus more for topping

Maple syrup for drizzling

Sliced strawberries for topping

Powdered sugar for dusting

Preheat a waffle iron.

In a large mixing bowl, whisk together the flour, sugar, baking powder, and salt. Add the buttermilk, eggs, vanilla extract, banana extract, and melted butter, and stir together until fully combined. Fold in the chocolate chips, butterscotch chips, and walnuts and stir until evenly distributed.

Using approximately ½ cup of batter per waffle, cook the waffles in the preheated waffle iron. (Total yield might vary slightly depending on the style of iron.)

Serve hot, each topped with a pat of butter, maple syrup, sliced strawberries, walnuts, and a touch of powdered sugar.

AMANDA'S GRIEF BISCUITS

When my dear friend, Amanda, experienced a tragic loss, she discovered that there was no road map for moving through grief, but there was magic to moving her hands. She found herself baking biscuits . . . and more biscuits . . . and even more biscuits. Baking became her therapy because it gave her steps to follow, and sitting still wasn't an option. I wanted to include this recipe, not only as an example of the healing power of baking, but also because these are mighty fine biscuits. White Lily flour is the key to this recipe, but if you can't get your hands on it, you can substitute 2½ cups cake flour, 2½ teaspoons baking powder, and ½ teaspoon salt.

 *Makes 8 biscuits*

2½ cups White Lily flour (or see substitution above), plus more for dusting

½ cup (1 stick) unsalted butter, frozen

1 cup buttermilk

Preheat the oven to 475°F. Line a baking sheet with parchment paper.

Measure 2 cups of the flour into a mixing bowl. Using a hand grater, grate the frozen stick of butter into the flour. Lightly stir to combine and then place the bowl in the refrigerator for 10 minutes. (Cold ingredients + hot oven = best fluff to the biscuit!) Remove from the fridge and create a well in the center of the butter and flour mixture. Pour in the buttermilk and stir it 15 times.

Transfer the dough to a floured surface and flatten it into an inch-thick rectangle. Fold the dough in half and press into another inch-thick rectangle. Repeat this 5 times to create those delicious, flaky layers.

Dip your biscuit cutter in flour and press it into the dough to cut out a biscuit. Try not to twist the cutter, as this will affect how much your biscuits rise. Flouring the cutter before you cut out each biscuit will help. Place the biscuits close together on the prepared baking sheet.

Bake for 13 to 15 minutes, until golden brown.

Serve hot, topped with butter and honey, honey.

SWEET AND SPICY CORN MUFFINS

The combination of savory, sweet, and spicy in these muffins make them a great addition to your breakfast spread, or a delicious option for a grab-n-go snack. And, if you can't stand the heat, don't get out of the kitchen; just eliminate the red pepper flakes!

Makes 12 muffins

2 cups all-purpose flour

1 cup cornmeal

1 cup sugar

½ cup packed light brown sugar

1 tablespoon baking powder

½ teaspoon baking soda

1 teaspoon table salt

1 tablespoon crushed red pepper flakes

4 extra-large eggs

1 cup whole milk

2 teaspoons pure vanilla extract

¾ cup (1½ sticks) unsalted butter, melted and cooled

Preheat the oven to 350°F.

In a large mixing bowl, whisk together the cornmeal, flour, sugar, brown sugar, baking powder, baking soda, salt, and crushed red pepper.

Add the eggs, milk, and vanilla extract and whisk together until fully combined. Fold in the melted butter. Carefully stir until just combined. Be careful not to overmix.

Line a muffin tin with paper baking cups or spray with nonstick cooking spray. Using an ice cream scoop or large spoon, distribute the batter evenly among the 12 muffin cups.

Bake for 20 to 25 minutes, until golden brown around the edges and lightly browned on top; a toothpick inserted into the center should come out clean.

Top with butter and a little drizzle of honey, and honey, you are in for a treat!

Store in an airtight container at room temperature for up to 4 days or freeze for up to a month.

LEMON POPPY SEED MUFFINS

I dream about these muffins. A little bit of lemon improves everything, and these muffins are no exception. The slightly crisp muffin top and soft inside crackle with piquancy but won't make your mouth pucker.

Makes 12 muffins

FOR THE MUFFINS:

3 cups all-purpose flour

½ cup sugar

½ cup packed light brown sugar

1 tablespoon baking powder

½ teaspoon baking soda

1 teaspoon salt

2 tablespoons poppy seeds

1½ cups sour cream

2 tablespoons fresh lemon juice

1 tablespoon lemon zest

2 extra-large eggs

½ cup (1 stick) unsalted butter, melted and cooled

FOR THE GLAZE:

1½ cups powdered sugar

3 tablespoons fresh lemon juice

1 tablespoon maple syrup

1 teaspoon pure vanilla extract

To make the muffins: Preheat the oven to 375°F.

In a large mixing bowl, whisk together the flour, sugar, brown sugar, baking powder, baking soda, salt, and poppy seeds. Set aside.

In a medium mixing bowl, combine the sour cream, lemon juice, lemon zest, and eggs and whisk together until smooth. Fold the wet mixture into the dry mixture, followed by the butter. Carefully stir until just combined. Be careful not to overmix.

Line a muffin tin with paper baking cups or spray the cups with nonstick baking spray. Using an ice cream scoop or large spoon, distribute the batter evenly among the 12 muffin cups.

Bake for 20 to 25 minutes, until golden brown around the edges and lightly browned on top; a toothpick inserted into the center should come out clean.

To make the glaze: In a small mixing bowl, whisk together the powdered sugar, lemon juice, maple syrup, and vanilla extract until fully combined and smooth.

When the muffins are cool, remove them from the pan and drizzle with the glaze. Allow the glaze to set and serve!

Store in airtight container at room temperature for up to 4 days or freeze for up to a month.

Acknowledgments

They say "it takes a village," and this entrepreneurial endeavor of Milk Jar Cookies is no exception. I have always been a very lucky person to have an incredible support system, and I couldn't be more grateful for that. While I want to sincerely say "thank you to everyone who has ever helped me, supported me, encouraged me, and contributed to who I am," I will also get a little more specific.

I want to start by thanking my family. I would not be where I am without you, and the journey would have been a lot less fun. To my mom and dad, thank you for giving me grit and raising me to dream big, work hard, love deeply, be bold, and approach everything I do with passion and purpose. It's easier to believe in myself because you believe in me so fiercely. To my brother and sister, thank you for being so supportive, willing to talk through business challenges, providing inspiration of all kinds, and always making me laugh harder than anyone else I know. To Kristie, Leo, and Jamie, our family unit was finally complete once you joined it. I love you all so much and couldn't be prouder to be a Cowan. And to the Wickers and extended Cowans, thank you for your love and support and always being the loudest cheering section anywhere. I love you.

To my in-laws, Ingrid and Jeff, thank you for believing in this dream of mine and supporting it with every ounce of your being. From demolition of an old Quiznos to building boxes and making deliveries, you are always at the ready to help. I promise we'll have new merch soon so you can have other shirts and hats to sport on your global adventures. I am incredibly grateful to have married into your family and love you so very much.

To Ashley Maxwell, thank you for going on this journey with me and contributing your incredible talent to make this book look the way it does. I am in awe of the beauty of these photographs. Thank you for making the sixteen-hour shoot days so much fun—I will never forget this experience and will treasure those times together.

To my agent, Carla Glasser, thank you for finding me and ushering this cookbook dream into reality. Your support and guidance is invaluable, and I look forward to future projects together.

To Shubhani Sarkar, the incredibly talented designer of this book, thank you for elevating every vision I had, and then some. To have someone of your caliber on this project is a dream come true, and I'm so grateful for your beautiful work.

To the wonderful team at Rizzoli, THANK YOU for believing in this project and providing me the opportunity to share this book with the world. This experience has been a true joy, and I feel very lucky to work with such a supportive publisher.

To Tate Hanyok, thank you for your energy, styling help, and 1,978 runs to the grocery store during the shoot. You are a gem of a human, and I am so glad to be your friend.

To all of our customers, thank you for your patronage, loyalty, and evangelism. I get to do what I love because of you, and it is an honor to be your cookie shop of choice. The smiles on your faces are what keep me going.

To the employees of Milk Jar Cookies, past, present, and future, THANK YOU. Your work every day to serve our customers is the lifeblood of this business. Each of you has contributed to the growth and success we've had, and I thank you.

To my incredible friends, thank you for being my extended family. Thank you for your love and support and cheering Milk Jar on for all these years. Thank you for understanding when the demands of the business keep me from seeing you. Thank you for lending a hand when needed and for reminding me to celebrate the wins, big and small.

To Charlie, I will love and miss you forever.

And last, but most, to my husband, Adam, thank you for your unwavering support, tireless work in and out of the shop, and lending your design talents to crafting the Milk Jar Cookies brand. I could not have done this without you. You said in your vows that you would support all of my dreams, cookie or otherwise, and you have done that, and then some. I square o forever.

Index

(Page references in *italics* refer to illustrations.)

A

almonds, in Rocky Road Cookies, 35–36, 37
apple:
  Oatmeal Cookies, 69–70, 71
  Pie, 125

B

Bacon Cheddar Scones, 169–70
baking sheets and pans, 13
banana:
  Cookies, Chocolate-Covered, 60, 61–62
  Nut Bread, Aunt Suz's, 163–64, *165*
  Pudding with Vanilla Wafer Cookies, 144–46, *145*
  Split Cookies, 29–30, *31*
  Split Puppy Chow, 136, *137*
  Split Waffles, *178,* 179
berries:
  Mixed Berry Pie, 121–22, *123*
  see also specific berries
Better Than Almost Anything Cake, 97–98, *99*
Birthday Cookies, *32,* 34
biscuits:
  Grief, Amanda's, 180, *181*
  Strawberry Shortcake, 111–12, *113*
blueberry(ies):
  Compote, 175, *177*
  Lemon Cookies, *78,* 79–80

Mixed Berry Pie, 121–22, *123*
Streusel Muffins, *166,* 167–68
bowls, mixing, 13
breads:
  Banana Nut, Aunt Suz's, 163–64, *165*
  Chocolate Chocolate Chip Zucchini, Mrs. Z's, *172,* 173–74
  Pumpkin, 157–58, *159*
breakfast bakes:
  Bacon Cheddar Scones, 169–70
  Banana Split Waffles, *178,* 179
  Cinnamon Rolls, Mama's, *160,* 161–62
  Grief Biscuits, Amanda's, 180, *181*
  Lemon Ricotta Pancakes with Blueberry Compote, 175–76, *177*
  Sour Cream Coffee Cake, 154–56, *155*
  see also breads; muffins
Brownies, Perfectly Fudgy, *106,* 107
butter, 11
Butterfinger candy, in Picnic Cookies, *66,* 67–68
buttermilk, 11
butterscotch:
  chips, in Banana Split Cookies, 29–30, *31*
  chips, in Banana Split Puppy Chow, 136, *137*
  Pudding with Homemade Whipped Cream, 130–32, *131*
  Salted, Cookies, 45–46, *47*

C

cakes:
  Better Than Almost Anything, 97–98, *99*
  Carrot, with Cream Cheese Frosting, 103–4
  Cheesecake with Cherry Compote Topping, *108,* 109–10
  Chocolate, with Chocolate Fudge Frosting, Your New Favorite, 91–93
  Chocolate Chip Cookie, 94–96, *95*
  Confetti, with White Frosting, *100,* 101–2
  German Chocolate, with Coconut Pecan Frosting, Hazel's, *114,* 115–17
candy cane, crushed, in Peppermint Bark Cookies, 87–88, *89*
Cap'n Crunch cereal, in Milk and Cereal Cookies, 75–76, 77
Caramel Chocolate Pecan Cookies, *42,* 43–44
Carrot Cake with Cream Cheese Frosting, 103–4
cereal:
  and Milk Cookies, 75–76, 77
  Rice Krispies, in PB&J Krispy Treats, 140, *141*
  Special K, in Hoosier Haystacks, *138,* 139
Cheddar Bacon Scones, 169–70
Cheesecake with Cherry Compote Topping, *108,* 109–10
Cherry Compote Topping, *108,* 109–10

chocolate:
Better Than Almost Anything
Cake, 97–98, 99
Brownies, Perfectly Fudgy, 106,
107
Cake with Chocolate Fudge
Frosting, Your New
Favorite, 91–93
Chocolate Chip Cookies,
23–24, 25
cocoa powder, 11–12
-Covered Banana Cookies, 60,
61–62
-Covered Pretzels, 142, 143
-Covered Strawberry Cookies,
84, 85–86
Fudge, 150, 151
Fudge Frosting, 92–93
German, Cake with Coconut
Pecan Frosting, Hazel's,
114, 115–17
Mint Cookies, 48, 49–50
Pecan Caramel Cookies, 42,
43–44
Pudding with Crème de la
Cloud, 133–35, 134
Raspberry Cookies, 23
Rocky Road Cookies, 35–36,
37
see also white chocolate
chocolate chip(s), 11
Banana Split Cookies, 29–30,
31
Banana Split Puppy Chow, 136,
137
Chocolate Zucchini Bread, Mrs.
Z's, 172, 173–74
Cookie Cake, 94–96, 95
Cookies, 14, 15–16
Cookies, Chocolate, 23–24, 25
Cookies, Inside-Out, 23, 25
Peppermint Bark Cookies,
87–88, 89
Picnic Cookies, 66, 67–68
Rocky Road Cookies, 35–36,
37
Walnut Cookies, 21–22
cinnamon:
-Infused Whipped Cream, 132
Rolls, Mama's, 160, 161–62

Sugar Cookies, 32, 33–34
cocoa powder, 11–12
coconut:
Carrot Cake with Cream
Cheese Frosting, 103–4
Pecan Frosting, 114, 117
Coffee Cake, Sour Cream,
154–56, 155
Confetti Cake with White Frosting,
100, 101–2
cookies:
Apple Oatmeal, 69–70, 71
Banana Split, 29–30, 31
Birthday, 32, 34
Chocolate Chip, 14, 15–16
Chocolate Chip Walnut, 21–22
Chocolate Chocolate Chip,
23–24, 25
Chocolate-Covered Banana,
60, 61–62
Chocolate-Covered
Strawberry, 84, 85–86
Chocolate Pecan Caramel, 42,
43–44
Chocolate Raspberry, 23
Cinnamon Sugar, 32, 33–34
English Toffee, 72, 73–74
Inside-Out Chocolate Chip,
23, 25
Key Lime Pie, 51–52, 53
Lemon Blueberry, 78, 79–80
Milk and Cereal, 75–76, 77
Mint Chocolate, 48, 49–50
Oatmeal Raisin, 38, 39–40,
41
Peach Cobbler, with Streusel
Topping, 81–82, 83
Peanut Butter, 63–64, 65
Peppermint Bark, 87–88, 89
Picnic, 66, 67–68
Pumpkin Pie, 57–58
Rocky Road, 35–36, 37
Salted Butterscotch, 45–46,
47
Vanilla Wafer, 146
Waffle, 54, 55–56
White Chocolate Macadamia,
26, 27–28
White Chocolate Raspberry,
17–18, 19

Corn Muffins, Sweet and Spicy,
182, 183
Cream Cheese Frosting, 104
Crème de la Cloud, 134, 135

E

eggs, 12
English Toffee Cookies, 72, 73–74
equipment, 13
extracts:
flavored, 12
vanilla, 13

F

flour, 12
frostings:
Chocolate Fudge, 92–93
Coconut Pecan, 114, 117
Cream Cheese, 104
White, 100, 102
Fruity Pebbles cereal, in Milk and
Cereal Cookies, 75–76, 77
Fudge, Chocolate, 150, 151
Frosting, 92–93
Fudgy Brownies, Perfect, 106, 107

G

German Chocolate Cake with
Coconut Pecan Frosting,
Hazel's, 114, 115–17
gluten-free flour, 12
gluten-free versions:
Chocolate Chip Cookie Cake,
94–96, 95
Chocolate Chip Cookies, 14,
15–16
Lemon Blueberry Cookies, 78,
79–80
Peppermint Bark Cookies,
87–88, 89
Salted Butterscotch Cookies,
45–46, 47
Golden Grahams cereal, in Milk
and Cereal Cookies,
75–76, 77
Grief Biscuits, Amanda's, 180, 181

H

Hoosier Haystacks, *138,* 139

I

ingredients, 11–13
Inside-Out Chocolate Chip
    Cookies, 23, *25*

K

Key Lime Pie Cookies, 51–52, *53*
Krispy Treats, PB&J, 140, *141*

L

lemon:
    Blueberry Cookies, *78,* 79–80
    Poppy Seed Muffins, 184–86,
        185
    Ricotta Pancakes with
        Blueberry Compote,
        175–76, *177*
Lucky Charms cereal, in Milk and
    Cereal Cookies, 75–76,
    77

M

Macadamia White Chocolate
    Cookies, *26,* 27–28
marshmallows:
    Chocolate Fudge, 150, *151*
    PB&J Krispy Treats, 140, *141*
    Rocky Road Cookies, 35–36,
        37
Marshmallows (recipe), 147–49,
    148
Milk and Cereal Cookies, 75–76,
    77
mint:
    Chocolate Cookies, *48,* 49–50
    Peppermint Bark Cookies,
        87–88, *89*
mixers, stand, 13
mixing bowls, 13

muffins:
    Blueberry Streusel, *166,*
        167–68
    Corn, Sweet and Spicy, *182,*
        183
    Lemon Poppy Seed, 184–86,
        185

N

no bake treats:
    Banana Split Puppy Chow, 136,
        137
    Chocolate-Covered Pretzels,
        142, 143
    Chocolate Fudge, 150, *151*
    Hoosier Haystacks, *138,* 139
    Marshmallows, 147–49, *148*
    PB&J Krispy Treats, 140, *141*
    see also puddings

O

oatmeal:
    Apple Cookies, 69–70, *71*
    Raisin Cookies, *38,* 39–40, *41*

P

Pancakes, Lemon Ricotta, with
    Blueberry Compote,
    175–76, *177*
parchment paper, 13
PB&J Krispy Treats, 140, *141*
Peach Cobbler Cookies with
    Streusel Topping, 81–82,
    83
peanut butter, 12–13
    chips, in Picnic Cookies, *66,*
        67–68
    Cookies, 63–64, *65*
    Hoosier Haystacks, *138,* 139
    PB&J Krispy Treats, 140, *141*
pecan(s):
    Banana Nut Bread, Aunt Suz's,
        163–64, *165*
    Candied, Topping, Pumpkin Pie
        Cookies with, 57–58

Chocolate Caramel Cookies,
    42, 43–44
Coconut Frosting, *114,* 117
Pie, *128,* 129
Peppermint Bark Cookies, 87–88,
    89
Picnic Cookies, *66,* 67–68
Piecrust, Perfect, *118,* 119–20
pie pans, 13
pies:
    Apple, 125
    Mixed Berry, 121–22, *123*
    Pecan, *128,* 129
    Pumpkin, 126–27, *127*
pistachio nuts, in Key Lime Pie
    Cookies, 51–52, *53*
Poppy Seed Lemon Muffins,
    184–86, *185*
potato chips, in Picnic Cookies,
    66, 67–68
pretzels:
    Chocolate-Covered, *142,*
        143
    Picnic Cookies, *66,* 67–68
puddings:
    Banana, with Vanilla Wafer
        Cookies, 144–46, *145*
    Butterscotch, with Homemade
        Whipped Cream, 130–
        32, *131*
    Chocolate, with Crème de la
        Cloud, 133–35, *134*
    Tapioca, *152,* 153
pumpkin:
    Bread, 157–58, *159*
    Pie, 126–27, *127*
    Pie Cookies, 57–58

R

rainbow nonpareils, in Birthday
    Cookies, *32,* 34
Raisin Oatmeal Cookies, *38,*
    39–40, *41*
raspberry(ies):
    Chocolate Cookies, 23
    Mixed Berry Pie, 121–22, *123*
    preserves, in PB&J Krispy
        Treats, 140, *141*

White Chocolate Cookies,
17–18, *19*
Rice Chex, in Banana Split Puppy
Chow, 136, *137*
Rice Krispies cereal:
Milk and Cereal Cookies,
75–76, *77*
PB&J Krispy Treats, 140, *141*
Ricotta Lemon Pancakes with
Blueberry Compote,
175–76, *177*
Rocky Road Cookies, 35–36, *37*
Rolo candies, in Chocolate Pecan
Caramel Cookies, *42,*
43–44

S

Salted Butterscotch Cookies,
45–46, *47*
Scones, Bacon Cheddar, 169–70
Shortcake, Strawberry, 111–12,
113
shortening, 13
Sour Cream Coffee Cake, 154–
56, *155*
Special K cereal, in Hoosier
Haystacks, *138,* 139
stand mixers, 13
strawberry(ies):
Banana Split Cookies, 29–30,
31
Cookies, Chocolate-Covered,
84, 85–86
freeze-dried, in Banana Split
Puppy Chow, 136, *137*
Mixed Berry Pie, 121–22, *123*
Shortcake, 111–12, *113*

streusel (topping):
Blueberry Muffins, *166,*
167–68
Peach Cobbler Cookies with,
81–82, *83*
Sour Cream Coffee Cake,
154–56, *155*

T

tapioca pearls, 13
Tapioca Pudding, *152,* 153
Thin Mints, in Mint Chocolate
Cookies, *48,* 49–50
toffee:
chips, in Better Than Almost
Anything Cake, 97–98,
99
English, Cookies, *72,* 73–74

V

vanilla extract, 13
Vanilla Wafer Cookies, 146

W

Waffle Cookies, *54,* 55–56
Waffles, Banana Split, *178,*
179
walnut(s):
Banana Split Cookies, 29–30,
31
Banana Split Puppy Chow, 136,
137
Carrot Cake with Cream
Cheese Frosting, 103–4

Chocolate Chip Cookies,
21–22
Chocolate Fudge, 150, *151*
Whipped Cream, 132
Cinnamon-Infused, 132
white chocolate:
chips, in Inside-Out Chocolate
Chip Cookies, 23, *25*
chips, in Key Lime Pie Cookies,
51–52, *53*
chips, in Peppermint Bark
Cookies, 87–88, *89*
Macadamia Cookies, *26,*
27–28
Raspberry Cookies, 17–18, *19*
White Frosting, *100,* 102
whole wheat flour, in Chocolate
Chocolate Chip Zucchini
Bread, Mrs. Z's, *172,*
173–74

Y

yogurt chips, 13
Milk and Cereal Cookies,
75–76, 77
Peach Cobbler Cookies with
Streusel Topping, 81–82,
83

Z

Zucchini Bread, Chocolate
Chocolate Chip, Mrs. Z's,
172, 173–74

To Adam,

For believing in me, even when I didn't.
I love you.

MILK JAR COOKIES BAKEBOOK
Cookies, Cakes, Pies, and More for Celebrations and Every Day
by Courtney Cowan

First published in the United States of America in 2020 by
Welcome Books, an imprint of Rizzoli International Publications, Inc.
300 Park Avenue South
New York, NY 10010
rizzoliusa.com

Copyright © 2020 by Courtney Cowan
milkjarcookies.com

Photography by Ashley Maxwell
ashleymaxwellphoto.com

"The Baker" courtesy of the Author

PUBLISHER: Charles Miers
EDITOR: Jono Jarrett
COVER AND INTERIOR DESIGN: Shubhani Sarkar, sarkardesignstudio.com
PRODUCTION MANAGER: Colin Hough-Trapp
MANAGING EDITOR: Lynn Scrabis

Printed in China

2020 2021 2022 2023 / 10 9 8 7 6 5 4 3 2 1

ISBN: 978-1-5996-2150-0
Library of Congress Control Number: 2020935850

VISIT US ONLINE:
Facebook.com/RizzolNewYork
Twitter: @Rizzoli_Books
Instagram.com/RizzoliBooks
Pinterest.com/RizzoliBooks
Youtube.com/user/RizzoliNY
Issuu.com/Rizzoli